T0332407

Earmarked for Collision

Collage art and film date back to the early 20th century (the earliest collages have roots in 12th-century Japan). It was rooted in the age of consumerism where artists addressed an array of political and social issues by creating a carefully crafted collision of pre-existing images and sounds to generate new meanings and commentaries on the surrounding world.

Collage has also pushed the boundaries of animation, by incorporating other artistic forms (e.g., photography, live action, experimental cinema, literature, found sound) while exploring an array of social, cultural and political issues.

In *Earmarked for Collision*, award-winning writer Chris Robinson (*The Animation Pimp*, *Mad Eyed Misfits*, *Unsung Heroes of Animation*) takes us on a tour of the history of collage animation, cataloguing the collage works of notable artists like Larry Jordan, Harry Smith, Stan Vanderbeek, Terry Gilliam, Janie Geiser, Martha Colburn, Lewis Klahr, Run Wrake, Lei Lei, Kelly Sears, Jodie Mack, and many, many others.

FOCUS ANIMATION Series

The Focus Animation Series aims to provide unique, accessible content that may not otherwise be published. We allow researchers, academics, and professionals the ability to quickly publish high impact, current literature in the field of animation for a global audience. This series is a fine complement to the existing, robust animation titles available through CRC Press/Focal Press.

Series Editor Chris Robinson is the Artistic Director of the Ottawa International Animation Festival (OIAF) and is a well-known figure in the animated film world. We welcome any submissions to help grow the wonderful content we are striving to provide to the animation community.

Earmarked for Collision
A Highly Biased Tour of Collage Animation

Chris Robinson

CRC Press
Taylor & Francis Group
Boca Raton London New York

CRC Press is an imprint of the
Taylor & Francis Group, an **informa** business

First edition published 2024
by CRC Press
6000 Broken Sound Parkway NW, Suite 300, Boca Raton, FL 33487-2742

and by CRC Press
4 Park Square, Milton Park, Abingdon, Oxon, OX14 4RN

CRC Press is an imprint of Taylor & Francis Group, LLC

ISBN: 9781032103129 (hbk)
ISBN: 9781032439082 (pbk)
ISBN: 9781003214724 (ebk)

DOI: 10.1201/9781003214724

Typeset in Times LT Std
by KnowledgeWorks Global Ltd.

never fixed, nor stable, but always just a passing, temporary energy-burst.

George Saunders, Lincoln in the Bardo

For Robert Pollard, whose soul-swirling music, art, and lyrics guided me (back) to the beauty, mischievousness, and fun of – among other things – collage art in all its forms.

Contents

Contents

Author Bio

Chris Robinson is a Canadian writer and author. He is also the Artistic Director of the Ottawa International Animation Festival (OIAF) and is a well-known figure in the animated film world. In 2020, he was awarded for Outstanding Contribution to Animation Studies by the World Festival of Animation Film – Animafest Zagreb. In 2022, he received the Rene Jodoin Prix for his contributions to Canadian animation.

Robinson has been called "one of the stylistically most original and most provocative experts in the history of animation". He made a name for himself with a unique and eclectic magazine column *Animation Pimp*, which became a book of the same name. He is a frequent contributor to Cartoon Brew and Animation World Magazine.

Mastering different methods and styles in critical and scholarly approaches, Robinson covers a broad range of Canadian and global subject matters in his books *Estonian Animation: Between Genius and Utter Illiteracy, Unsung Heroes of Animation, Canadian Animation: Looking for a Place to Happen, Ballad of a Thin Man: In Search of Ryan Larkin, Animators Unearthed*, and *Japanese Animation: Time Out of Mind*.

In addition to his writing on animation, Robinson also wrote the award-winning animated short, *Lipsett Diaries* (2010) directed by Theodore Ushev, a graphic novel, *My Balls Are Killing Me*, and a live-action feature script, *Idling*.

Breaking Stones with a Feather

Why Collage?

1

What have I gotten myself into?

Trying to define, compartmentalize, label, and pull together collage animation is akin to breaking a stone with a feather duster.

It's a fool's task.

Clearly, I'm a fool.

But why should this be easy? We're in an age of visual saturation, where images and sounds collide seemingly every second within our subconscious. Uniting a technique rooted in disruption, displacement, and destruction *should* be challenging.

While the animation industry salivates over every shiny new technological toy, it's an older, more traditional, and much less sexy technique that offers the aptest reflection of modern society: collage.

But just what the hell is collage?

Let's get a few things sorted before we proceed.

When I talk about collage animation, I am not necessarily talking about cut-out animation. Lotte Reiniger, for instance, made cut-out, not collage, films. She created her cut-out materials. The same goes with other artists and movies that appear to be collages: the Dutch father and son team, Paul and Menno de Nooijer, Jim Blashfield, or individual films like Jan Lenica's *Fantorro* (1973) and Zbigniew Rybczyński's Oscar-winner, *Tango* (1980). William Kentridge certainly incorporates collage into some of his work, but one would be hard pressed to say he is making collage animation films. In these cases, they use a mix of cut-out photo, xerox, or video imagery, but the difference is that those altered images are not heisted materials. Those artists created them specifically for their respective films. These works are closer to cut-out than my notion of collage.

DOI: 10.1201/9781003214724-1

Montage is more of a live-action cinema technique. Think Sergei Eisenstein, Esther Shub, Bruce Connor, Stan Brakhage, Soda Jerk, or Arthur Lipsett. Like collage, montage films take two seemingly disparate images and place them side by side to generate a new reaction or meaning. It's cool. It's like collage, but it's not animated (and let's not get into a whole "what is animation" debate here. I don't have time, okay?).

Décollage is kind of the opposite of collage. It means removing something, taking it off, ungluing, or ripping it off. Décollage was a widespread technique in the 1960s when artists would tear off elements of street posters or advertisements, leaving only selected texts or image portions. So it is like a collage in that you generate new meaning from stolen images, but it's generally taking all that material from a single ad or poster and working on that same canvas. (Oh, and if you want to go crazy, there are sub-forms of Décollage called Déchirage and Dépliage, but I'll leave that to you to explore.)

Assemblage is a 3D version of collage where the artist assembles an assortment of found objects. Some of Jan Svankmajer, The Quay Brothers, and parts of Jodie Mack's work certainly fall under this category.

Bricolage tends to be where the artist works with whatever materials are nearby.

The *photomontage* is closest to what I'm exploring in this book. This approach involves multiple photos (or illustrations) cut or torn apart and united into a new image.

And we can go on and on. There's compositing (a digital tool where multiple photos are combined to make a single picture) and digital collage (using your computer mouse to cut and paste along with assorted software, like Photoshop). And there are deep fake videos, memes, and gifs, which all use some elements of collage.

To make things somewhat simplistic, I'm defining collage animation as a technique where pre-existing or ready-made materials are heisted along with other unique materials to generate new meanings.

Collage is a collision of disparate materials, animated Frankensteins. It is taking all these "dead" bits, pieces, or fragments and breathing new life, purpose, and meaning into them. Collage is parasitic. It sponges, plunders, steals, and reworks.

Collage brings different realities together in the hopes of sparking a connection. It can build contradictions, erase identities, and form new ones. It rejects original intentions. A collage is a kaleidoscope or, rather, a "collideoscope" that dethrones time and space, which toys with your memory and perception by collapsing multiple views into one. You feel a snippet of recognition, but you need more to feel sure or comfortable. Collage disrupts you, me, and us. Like jazz, collage takes a melody from here, a melody from there, and tosses and turns it into a new song.

It's an art made by everyone, not one.

Oh, you want something more profound? Henri Bergson has said (he wasn't speaking about collage, but it certainly applies): "Many diverse images, borrowed from very different orders of things, may, by the convergence of their action, direct consciousness to the precise point where there is a certain intuition to be seized."[1]

There's something playful, violent, provocative, mysterious, and accessible about collage. Anyone can do it, and for the most part, most of us have done it, whether in the early years of school or at home with scrapbooks and photo albums. Collage also straddles many intersections, particularly between so-called high and low art, between professional and amateur. Picasso did it, and so did my grandma.

As a child (as I'm sure was the case with many of you), one of my first encounters with art was cut and paste. I had, for example, a hockey scrapbook where I cut and pasted assorted images and texts from magazines and newspapers. I also cut and pasted my hockey cards to ensure that all trades and free agent signings were up to date. Why? I have no idea. It was a way to preserve, to make something that wasn't mine, my own. There could be something related to mortality with it all. A desperate desire to keep something from fading into oblivion?

Around age 9 or 10, I discovered collage animation – without knowing what it was – via Terry Gilliam and his cartoon segments for the TV series *Monty Python's Flying Circus*. For many of us of that generation, Gilliam's animation was also our introduction to more experimental animation styles, far removed from the safe and polished domains of Walt Disney, Warner Bros., and so much awful TV animation. Later, as a teenager, I was in local bands, and we (like almost everyone) made collage concert posters that cut and pasted images and letters and then xeroxed them together.

As a writer, I've always liked works that eschew categorization, that seamlessly blend fact and fiction. As I'll touch upon later in this book, those works often take you to a more profound truth than any fact alone could.

Beyond all those precious and likely faulty memories, there's just something deliciously destructive about collage. You get to rip, tear, or cut stuff up and piece it together into whatever you want.

Isn't that beautiful and liberating?

To be visually creative, you don't have to know how to draw or paint.

Strangely enough, given my 30-plus years of working in animation, I started paying closer attention to collage through music, specifically the work of Guided by Voices and the man behind them, Robert Pollard.

Pollard's songs are collages. He takes parts from various songs he's demoed and often combines them with other fragments to create new songs. He approaches lyric writing in a similar vein. Beyond that, he's also a collage artist who creates covers for many Guided by Voices records. I'm never quite sure what a Pollard song might mean, but he frequently leaves you with vague imprints or goosebumps open to a wealth of interpretations, all of which are correct.

It's a similar feeling to what I experienced from the collage work of Martha Colburn and Janie Geiser, who were the first collage animators to grab my attention.

Then, in 2018, while putting together a collage retrospective for the Ottawa International Animation Festival, I was surprised by the lack of critical and historical attention given to the collage technique. Collage animators are often lumped in with experimental cinema, the art gallery scene, or tossed in with other experimental animation techniques (i.e. cut-out animation). The substantial body of collage animation that's been made deserves wider recognition and a more cohesive focus.

Collage is ubiquitous these days. With the rise of digital technology and software tools like good ol' photoshop, mixing and matching imagery has become a standard. Every day we've got memes, deep fakes, A.I., and altered images. Since the 1990s, Machinima has enabled users to hijack and alter video game environments to create their works. Even mainstream Hollywood resurrects actors/characters using borrowed materials (e.g. *Rogue One, The Mandalorian*). Before that, vintage footage of Fred Astaire was altered and reused for a vacuum commercial. Collage expands well beyond the walls of visual art. In literature, collage or cut-up techniques were popularized by William S. Burroughs and Brion Gysin but were rooted in the Dada movement of the 1920s. Sampling and mash-ups (a collision of two songs) have been a decades-old mainstay. Collage elements are so dominant now that we don't know the real from the phony.

That's a long way from the anti-authoritarian roots of collage art. Let's agree that collage art initially sought to liberate art and the artist or was used to critique government and society. It now feels like it's gone in the opposite direction, used to confuse, lie, manipulate, and alter to reinforce the establishment.

Beyond that, the collage technique has also pushed the boundaries of animation by incorporating other artistic forms (e.g. photography, live action, experimental cinema, literature, found sound) while exploring various social, cultural, and political issues.

As you're thumbing these pages while scrolling on your phones, keep in mind that you're witnessing my journey of discovery with collage. I'm not an expert on collage art or collage animation. This book is a journey of joy and curiosity, an attempt to catalogue an assortment of animators from the 20th and 21st centuries who've consistently worked with collage materials. I hope this endeavour will encourage others to dive deeper and uncover more than I can manage in this book.

Some – including myself – will be frustrated by this book's lack of visual references. Fortunately, you can find many referenced films on Vimeo and YouTube.

ACKNOWLEDGEMENTS

First and foremost, I want to thank Robert Pollard and Sarah Zade-Pollard for the title of this book. You can find that splendid song on the album, *Let it Bleed* by Boston Spaceships.

Secondly, a big thanks to the late Giannalberto Bendazzi, who first supported this project.

Thirdly, my long-time friend and colleague, Gerben Schermer, graciously took time to read drafts, make comments, and dig out various films and voices that I'd initially overlooked.

And, of course, a massive thanks to all the folks who have given me oodles of their time and attention: Lewis Klahr, Jodie Mack, Lei Lei, Kathleen Quillian, Janie Geiser, Kelly Sears, Winston Hacking, Martha Colburn, Lawrence Jordan, Stacey Steers, Miwa Matreyek, Xander Marro, Frank Mouris, Jeanette Jeanenne, Marko Tadić, Dalibor Barić, Peter Tscherkassky, Jean-Thomas Bédard, Velislava Gospodinova, Jelena Popović, Harry Neall, Mak Peyre, Jarvis Neall, Annaida Orosz, Tamás Patrovits, Brigitta Iványi-Bitter, Jim Blashfield, Jean-Baptiste Garnero, Dina Goder, Steven Woloshen, Emma Calder, Lisa Barcy, Osbert Parker, Igor Prassel, Yiorgos Tsangaris, Marco de Blois, Thomas Corriveau, Devin Hartley, and Ben Compton.

If I missed someone, pretend your name is *here*.

NOTE

1   https://www.bard.edu/library/pdfs/archives/Bergson_Introduction_to_Metaphysics.pdf.

Umbrellas and Sewing Machines – A Brief Look at the History of Collage Art

2

Torn Formations

Long before it was even labelled collage, many folks were horsing around with the concept using various materials.

As far back as the 12 century, Japanese poets wrote on torn and pasted sheets of coloured paper. In 13th-century Persia, leatherworks used images and goatskin to make book bindings. They also used leaves and flowers. Before the 16th century, Europeans cut paper and parchment for coats of arms and assorted family badges and emblems. In the 16th century, you could buy a book that taught the art of cutout silhouettes or check out the feather-works made in Mexico. By the 17th century, there were corn kernel mosaics, while Nuns were into butterfly collages. In the 18th century, we saw the emergence of the family album with pasted pictures and cut-outs. And by the 19th century, schoolchildren in Germany began doing collage work. In that same century, promotional posters were created using collage materials (usually to promote theatre performances).

Photomontage also emerged in the 1800s, primarily for journalism, picture postcards, and commercial publicity. A Swedish photographer, O.G.

DOI: 10.1201/9781003214724-2

Rejnader, made a photo called *The Two Paths of Life* (1875), composed of about 30 different shots of people and backgrounds. A pharmacist even made woodcuts from the comics section of the paper.

The list goes on. There were paper collages and small pictures used in prayer books; hand-painted valentines decorated with pictures, lithographs, and engravings; and ashtrays with cigar bands around them. Even some coffins were covered with buttons, hooks, and ladies' garters.

Mass mechanical production gave rise to newspapers, photographs, advertisements, and postage stamps, triggering the increase of scrapbooking as a pastime, especially for upper-middle-class women in Europe and North America.

Until the second decade of the 20th century, collage was primarily a cross between craft, hobby, and folk art.

COLLAGE GOES BIG TIME

I'm not going to dive deeply into collage art here. Plenty of fine books detail the development and history of collage art. Go check them out. But here's a quickie summary of the evolution of collage through art and cinema.

For many, collage materials in fine art likely began between 1907 and 1912. Georges Braque and Pablo Picasso are generally credited as the pioneers of collage art, though no one has a clue who did it first. Both artists did a lot of work during that period that they didn't sign or date.

Legend has it that Picasso and Braque had been hanging out. After one of their social sessions, Braque allegedly walked past a wallpaper store, saw some faux wood-grain wallpaper, bought it, went home, and started pasting parts of the paper onto some charcoal drawings. *Fruit Dish and Glass* (1912) resulted from that collision. This collision will open up a new direction in art for Braque, Picasso, and a slew of artists. "After making the first *papier collé*, I felt a great shock, and it was an even greater shock for Picasso when I showed it to him," Braque recalled later.[1]

Soon enough, Picasso took an oilcloth, a chair caning design and a rope to create *Still Life with a Chair Caning* (1912). Picasso went nuts with collage, making hundreds of pieces until around 1915 when he just up and turned to other techniques. Picasso used everything: fabrics, metal, newspaper fragments, parts of musical instruments, music scores, tobacco boxes, etc. For these Cubist artists, using every day, ready-made objects were a new way of thinking about art, liberating them from the restrictions of painting. It was an eye-opening experience. Instead of pastoral landscapes, they found beauty in everyday materials: business signs, posters, shop windows, newspapers, advertisements, etc. This collision of materials reflected the surrounding political and social chaos: The Balkan Wars in 1912/1913, the breakout of the world war, Anti-semitism, and the rise of industry and consumerism.

With a world in chaos, collage was the ideal distorted mirror to reflect the global madness. By breaking apart materials, collage art forced artists and viewers to question the validity and wholeness of representation and reality.

Then as now, trends – good ones at least – become, you guessed it, trendy. Soon enough, other Parisian-based artists like Juan Gris, Umberto Boccioni, Carlo Carrà, Man Ray, and Giacomo Balla began doing collage works of their own. In relatively quick succession, the collage influence would travel the globe, influencing artists in the Dada, Russian Constructivism, Surrealism, and Pop Art movements right through to the digital age and the emergence of photocopiers and computers.

By the end of the decade, collage was embraced by German Dadaists like Karl Arp, Kurt Schwitters, Hannah Hoch, Raoul Hausmann, George Grosz, and John Heartfield. Collage and Dada were a perfect match. If the Marx Brothers hooked up with The Sex Pistols, Dada might have been the result: an absurd, anarchist-tinged rejection of contemporary social, political, and commercial culture. They mocked everything: war, politicians, patriotism, nationalism, and your mom.

Beyond pasting papers and various materials, the Dada collagists incorporated photos into the mix. They used collage elements to attack all forms of society, ridiculing politicians, and government, notably Hitler and his band of fascists. This use of photo fragments became known as photomontage, a word that John Heartfield claims to have invented. Heartfield saw collage as a way of rejecting the artist, authorship (given that we credit these folks for their respective works, that laudable intention failed miserably), and the precious nature of art, especially painting. For Heartfield, "the doll a child throws away, a brightly coloured scrap of cloth, are more essential expressions than those of all the jackasses who wish to transplant themselves for all eternity in oil paints into an endless number of front parlours."[2]

Hannah Höch, one of the few women in the sometimes misogynist Dada group, used pictures and texts taken from magazines and newspapers and reassembled them to comment on themes of gender, sexuality, and androgyny. Höch's work questioned prevailing sexist attitudes about women's roles in society.

Kurt Schwitters went even further with collage, using materials he'd find in the garbage or on the street. His works incorporated various found materials, including newspaper fragments, concert tickets, cigarette butts, bus tickets, and old wires.

The use of appropriated, ready-made materials (often ripped, literally, from newspapers and advertisements) by Dadaists took the piss on the importance of artistic skill while collapsing the boundaries between so-called high and low culture. Creating a collage was a rejection, a welcome collision of seemingly random encounters to disrupt the false homogeneity being peddled to people (e.g. the photograph was seen as a factual document of the world). The works were frequently shocking, violent, and unsettling. Today, of course, all those punk-ish themes have been dismantled by time. Messages once bold have now been hushed and forgotten, lost in the harsh storm of time and fluttered memories.

Enduring their own political and societal chaos, Russian artists were also attracted to collage, primarily for its violent nature (remember, collage is about collisions and clashes). The painting was too bourgeois, but the collage was more in line with the worker, the everyman. Even the notion of the artist was altered, with Constructivist artists viewing themselves as technicians or engineers. Constructivists were trying to fuse art and revolution. They wanted to create a new language that promoted the new era in Russian/Soviet socialist history.

The roots of Constructivism lead back to Vladimir Tatlin and Kazimir Malevich. Tatlin visited Picasso's Paris studio in 1913 and was smitten with the Spaniard's three-dimensional wooden pieces. From there, Tatlin and Malevich created their collage-inspired works. Talin made the assemblage piece, *Corner Counter Reliefs* (1915), while Malevich created *Lady at the Poster Column* (1914) using a combination of geometric fragments, photos, and snippets of text taken from Russian and French newspapers.

Soon artists like Alexander Rodchenko, The Stenberg Brothers, El Lissitzky, and others used a combination of words/letters, glass, wood, metal, photograph fragments, and geometric shapes to create posters that sought to communicate social and political concerns to the workers and women. For four years (1919–1922), these artists and others produced thousands of propaganda posters for various clients, including the state news agency, the Russian Telegraph Agency (ROSTA).

As we'll discuss, Constructivist collages soon made their way into the moving image via landmark filmmakers Ester Shub, Lev Kuleshov, Sergei Eisenstein, and Dziga Vertov.

The Surrealists jumped on board the collage train and took it on a wild ride. Surrealist artists used collage elements to create unusual, dream-like scenarios that explored automatism and stream of consciousness or, as Andre Breton described (19th-century poet Comte de Lautréamont). "the chance encounter or a sewing machine and an umbrella on an operating table."[3] He was describing surrealism, but that's a spot-on definition of collage. So, the surrealists were more interested in projecting the inner chaos of dreams and the subconscious rather than looking out at the world.

Surrealism also took collage in new directions. It was no longer limited to glue and paper or photomontages, etc. Max Ernst created three collage novels that combined verbal and visual pieces. Joseph Cornell made boxes with dream-like imagery taken from various found materials. Cornell's work would significantly influence one of the pioneers of collage animation, Larry Jordan.

Collage hit the U.S.A. in the early 40s. A year after the Americans entered WWII, Peggy Guggenheim opened her gallery, *The Art of This Century*, in Manhattan. Showcasing works by International artists (Arp, Braque, Dali, Ernst, Kandinsky, Picasso, etc.) alongside those of American artists (e.g. Alexander Calder, Jackson Pollock, Mark Rothko and even Robert De Niro's Dad), the Gallery played an enormous role in influencing art in New York.

Cornell and Laurence Vail's collage pieces and Marcel Duchamp's *Box-Valise* were among the works exhibited at the gallery. Duchamp collected a variety of his works (mixed media assemblage/collage of miniature replicas, photographs, and colour reproductions of his earlier works) and presented them inside a briefcase. A portable art gallery.

In 1945, the gallery organized the "Exhibition of Collage," featuring new works by Robert Motherwell, William Baziotes, Jackson Pollock, and his wife, Lee Krasner (who was better at collage than her famous and troubled husband). One imagines that collage was a form of therapy for Krasner. She was ripping and cutting up materials, likely providing solace from life with a volatile and insecure alcoholic.

Collage eventually made its way to the American West coast and certainly influenced Beat Culture and notably the cut-up writings of William S. Burroughs. In Los Angeles, artists like Wallace Berman and Clay Spohn (who had studied under Fernand Léger in Paris) made mixed-media and assemblage work. Bruce Connor was one of the emerging artists who would influence collage animators like Lewis Klahr. Connor made assemblage work using women's stockings, bicycle wheels, broken dolls, fur, fringe, costume jewelry, and candles, often combined with collaged or painted surfaces. Significant themes in Connor's work were the standard collage themes: consumerism, sexism, and the general awfulness of capitalism and disposable culture. Connor began making influential montage films in the 1950s.

Meanwhile, Pop Art started its engines in the United Kingdom before making its way to the U.S.A. With their love of the mass or junk culture like B-movies, tabloids, and assorted kitsch, collage and pop art were a match made in dissension heaven.

MONTAGE IN CINEMA

In terms of the moving image, we can point to Soviet artists like Ester Shub, Dsiga Vertov and, most famously, Sergei Eisenstein as notable practitioners of montage (placing two seemingly disconnected images side by side to create new and unexpected meanings/reactions). We can also go back even earlier to see a variation of montage being used. Georges Melies used compositing (using multiple exposures) as early as 1900. Buster Keaton used similar techniques in classics like *The Playground* (1921) and *Sherlock Jr.* (1924). In terms of collage, some point to Joseph Cornell's *Rose Hobart* (1936) as the first collage film (Cornell cut and re-edited a Hollywood film, *East of Borneo*, into a surrealist short).

Many works straddle the boundaries between film and animation, and it's crucial to mention montage artists like Bruce Connor, Arthur Lipsett, and Soda Jerk (the contemporary Australian duo who freely alter classic films). In most of those works, as necessary and influential as they are, one could argue that they are not animated; they are placing found images next to each other without using stop-motion. I admit that this is tricky territory that potentially does a disservice to animation by restricting what it can and cannot be.

Speaking of stop-motion, Ladislas Starewich's classic, *The Cameraman's Revenge* (1912), has elements of collage or assemblage. Starewich certainly did take found material (dead insects) and put them in an entirely new context. Hell, he gave them life again!

COLLAGE CO-OPTED

By the 1960s, the mainstream had co-opted collage. It was used regularly in television and print advertising. In truth, the commercial highjacking of collage had begun much earlier. Russian artists have used collages to promote government policies and the latest films. Collage was frequently used in advertising and war propaganda (e.g. a 1941 ad for photos of women alongside a giant carrot to promote refrigerators, while a 1942 War Bonds poster features pictures of two children with cut-out photos of gas masks covering their faces).

If you could take found images out of their original context to inspire an audience to think about the society they live in, then why not also use them to get them to buy stuff?

By the 1970s and 1980s, collage was either dead or reborn, depending on who you ask. Mass culture exploded everywhere, and new technologies (xerox machines, computers) opened the floodgates. You didn't need scissors and glue. Soon, all you needed was a computer, a keyboard, and a mouse to cut and paste.

And it makes sense that collage has become more prominent. Not only have digital technology tools made the arduous process more manageable, but we live in an age where we can manipulate and alter everything and anything (thanks to Photoshop). Alterations are commonplace now, used to make gifs, memes, and deep fakes. What magazine doesn't adjust a model's physical features to fit in with ridiculous notions of body image standards?

Today, collage is everywhere in this age of globalization and technical saturation. A machine gun of images, voices, and information is blasted across our brainscape before we have even a moment to contemplate them. We are so saturated with manipulated imagery, can collage even combat a world where images are being appropriated and distorted every second? The roots of collage art were linked with critiquing and deconstructing the prevailing values of society, with criticizing wars, technology, capitalism, communism, and all the damn isms. Has it changed anything? It was co-opted so quickly by commercial interests that it lost its defiant characteristics early on. Does collage have any real relevance anymore? Has it just returned to its hobby roots, made for personal pleasure, or does collage remain a vital weapon for fighting those who distort the world for rather nefarious purposes?

I don't know the answer.

NOTES

1 https://magazine.artland.com/the-history-of-collage-art/.
2 *Collage*, Herta Wescher. New York: Harry N.Abrams, 1978, p. 21.
3 *Mad Love* by André Breton, Lincoln, NE: Bison Books, 1988, p. 123.

Fist Fights, Alchemists, Magicians and Python

1950s/1960s

3

Before we start, a few words about the book's structure. I am following a very loose chronological order based on when the featured animator first started doing collage works. So, even though, for example, Larry Jordan continues to make films, his use of collage begins in the 1960s. Lewis Klahr made collage films from the 1980s to the present time, but I've placed it in the 1970s/80s section to coincide with the time of his first collage films.

Initially, I intended to include an assortment of "Hit Singles" segments throughout the book. These segments acknowledge examples of collage animations made by artists who primarily worked with other techniques. However, space limitations forced me to ditch that idea. It is still worth acknowledging this mere sampler of collage films: Mothlight (Stan Brakhage, 1963), the "Eleanor Rigby" segment from Yellow Submarine (George Dunning, 1968), Butterfly (Peter Brouwer, 1973), Koko (George Griffin, 1988), Superhero (Emily Breer, 1995), Fast Film (Virgil Widrich, 2003), Lipsett Diaries (Theodore Ushev, 2010), Windows (Angella Lipskaya, 2015), and an assortment of Hungarian collage animation commercials made in the 1960s and 1970s.

DOI: 10.1201/9781003214724-3   15

ROBERT BREER (U.S.A.)

The first animated collage film (until someone corrects me) was Robert Breer's *Un Miracle* (1954) – a collaboration with Pontus Hultén, the Swedish curator who served as the director of the Pompidou Centre from 1973 to 1981. *Un Miracle* is an outstanding debut. It's short, funny, and profane. Standing in an open window before an enthusiastic audience, Pope Pius XII starts juggling three red balls. Soon one of the balls is replaced by his head. Finally, head on upside down, he rises to the heavens (or maybe just the ceiling of his pad). In just over a minute, Breer creates an anarchistic, absurd work with a little bit of anti-Church venom (Pope Pius XII was allegedly a tad anti-Semetic with fascist leanings). For Breer, "it was called the funniest film in the world ever made" or something like that. Lasts 30 seconds. Not funny anymore, but in those days, collage was new.[1] Although short and somewhat minimalist, *Un Miracle* takes photomontage elements of Dada collages while anticipating the work of Stan VanDerBeek and Terry Gilliam, among others.

Breer was never strictly a collage artist, and *Un Miracle* might be the only example of full-on collage animation he ever did. Still, he incorporated collage elements (often mixed with drawings and rotoscope) in many of his works, notably *Recreation* (1956–1957), *Fist Fight* (1964), *Jamestown Balloos* (1957), *LMNO* (1978), Bang (1986), Time Flies (1997), and his final works, ATOZ (2000). Breer likened his works to "a sort of stew: once in a while, something recognizable comes to the surface and disappears again."[2]

Recreation uses an assortment of elements: objects, paper cut-outs, fragments of posters, catalogues, and ads. It's two collages in one: there's a visual element and then an odd fragmented text read in French. Unlike *Un Miracle*, Breer doesn't give a centre, and there's nothing to grab hold of here. Images and words race by before we can process what we just saw. The title perfectly reflects the nature of collage (to recreate), but it also demonstrates the playfulness of Breer's work. Unlike many heavy-handed experimental films, Breer's work almost always avoids becoming too serious.

Jamestown Balloos is a three-part film. The first and final parts are in black and white with sound, while the middle section is silent and in colour. An anti-war theme is readily apparent, given the military drum beat alongside the cut-out photos of soldiers, historical figures (notably, Napoleon), tanks, and various war-related materials. There's even a satirical play on masculinity: boys swept into war, cut-out figures of soldiers in cut-off clothes looking more like magazine models. Part 2 offers a respite as the war drums stop while watercolour images flash on the screen. Is this a period of peace or a struggle between peace and violence? The off-season of war? Soon enough, part 3 begins, and we're back to the pounding drums, soldiers, and tanks. *Jamestown* would be the last time Breer explored collage animation in such a detail.

Fist Fight, which resembles the found footage films of Arthur Lipsett, is closer to montage, with an assortment of photographs, drawn animations, cartoons, playing cards, textures and geometric shapes coming and going, alongside bursts of drawings and found objects. *Fist Fight* is like a chaotic flip book with no apparent narrative or set theme. Like many of Breer's films, viewing *Fist Fight* is like watching life flash before your eyes. It just flies by, and you've no clue what happened. You're left stunned and mystified. You feel something, but you need to figure out what.

After *Fist Fight*, photos or outright collage elements take more of a backseat in his films. *LMNO*, *Bang*, and *Time Flies*, among others, all incorporate collage elements, but these works are dominated more by drawings and rotoscoped imagery. Still, if we follow the idea of collage as a collision, then many of Breer's films fall into the ballpark of collage, even when using rotoscope and drawings. "I thought in terms of collage, of fragments, so that this shape wasn't complete without the other one. I was making a family of shapes, and families are kind of incomplete. You know, an individual in a family is somewhat more complete with the other members around, right? I don't know if that holds up but at least one shape .... If I made the shape that took care of that, I wouldn't make another one slightly different."[3]

HARRY SMITH (U.S.A.)

After Breer got the ball rolling with collage animation, the late 1950s saw a mini-explosion in the use of collage elements. Next comes the eccentric Harry Smith, whose entire life was like a collage. He was a filmmaker, magician, artist, hoarder, mystic, alchemist, alcoholic, and borderline psychopath. He saw himself simply as an archeologist.

He was deeply influenced by Dada and Surrealism and particularly the collage work of Max Ernst. Like Georges Melies, Smith was into magic and saw film as a great avenue to explore illusions.

Smith is most famous for his extraordinary Anthology of Folk Music collection), but he was so much more than that. He made animation films for a period of his life (mainly in the 1950s). His initial works were cameraless, paint-on-film ones before he switched to collage films in 1957. Not one for fancy titles, his collage films were simply named *Film No. 8* (which has been lost but was a black and white film *Black and white collage using cut-outs from 19th-Century ladies' wear catalogues and elocution books*), *No. 9* (which I cannot locate, but combines old biology books alongside temperance posters), *10*, and *11*. Then there is the opus, *No. 12*, a feature-length film known as *Heaven and Earth Magic*. No one can pinpoint precise years, but they were likely made in the late 1950s.

Smith's films are deeply rooted in alchemy and the surreal. In all his works, chance and improvisation lead the way more than a pre-planned vision.

No. 10 – Mirror Animations

Falling snowflakes transform into a burst of kaleidoscopic colours and shapes. Birds, bones, and eyes balls emerge. A skeletal figure is formed and soon transforms into a young warrior-like skeletal figure who soon rises out of a box he was first created within. An insect-like figure emerges and frantically roams around the four walls of the box before a football and ball appear. In a flash, they transform into some minotaur-like demon figure. A serpent seems to be followed by a parade of objects: cut-out dolls, watches, and eyeballs.

I could go on, but I won't. Best you seek the film out yourself, sit back, relax, and go for a ride. No amount of description satisfactorily captures the spirit of this mysterious, freewheeling work. We're in a land of gods, demons, goddesses, good and evil entwined in mystical dance.

Smith draws from a slew of seemingly incompatible sources (taken from his vast collection; these days we'd be deeming him a hoarder): ancient religious figures and symbols mixed with more modern images of a football, a postman, and a children's toy wagon.

As critic P. Adams Sitney (who, in 1973, wrote the most thorough piece to date on the goings-on in Smith's work) notes:

> A detailed description of these films, short as they are, would require a volume. So many fleeting collages are composed of internal subcollages, often associated with a single shape, the iconography of different cultures. It would need several pages to describe each one's presence—which lasts on the screen perhaps a second—before one could go on to the shape it changes into, which of course, would also have its subdivisions.[4]

No. 11 – Mirror Animations

An extension of *No. 10*, *No. 11* is like a remix of its predecessor or, say, a different take. Like *#10*, this one begins with falling snowflakes. This time, the image gives way to an angel or priestess dressed in white who holds, maybe, a planet above her head. Lines or beams of colour appear behind her as a fish swims by. She is beckoning an assortment of images with simple hand gestures. From there, we see a ballerina and a postman (who appeared in *No. 10*). They dance in that familiar box we saw in the previous film. There's a basketball, a Persian rug, the red wagon, and football again, a Hindu figure, and a wall of glittering circles. If there is a common theme beyond the recurring images, it's a sense of mortality. In both films, a skeletal figure is prominent. Are we in an afterlife? A pre-existence? It's hard to say. *No. 11* has a more leisurely pace, highlighted by Thelonious Monk's song, "Misterioso." It adds a soft, chill vibe to Smith's beautiful imagery. And whatever meanings you want to lift from the film, there's no mistaking the utter beauty of the imagery created through shapes, colours, and framing.

As Simon Reynolds observes, Smith's collage films were born from his obsessive collection of material, primarily 19th-century illustrations:

> He filed the cut-outs – photographs or drawings of people, animals, vegetables, tools, furniture, and sundry other objects - in glassine envelopes for protection while noting on file cards every possible interaction a given image could have with another image. Yet, contradicting all this obsessive-compulsive preparation, Smith aimed for a state of mental vacancy akin to automatic writing when it came to the assembly process.[5]

No. 12 (Heaven and Earth Magic)

Smith's most ambitious and challenging work (apparently, the feature version that exists is merely a fragment of his original intention) is *No. 12*. I am figuring out how to summarize the film: There's something about a lady chasing a dog that has taken off with her watermelon. After, she visits the dentist and then hallucinates while drugged up. She may go to Heaven, Israel, or Montreal during her "trip." Eventually, she comes back down to earth.

No. 12 is so dense that Nos *10* and *11* seem almost accessible by comparison. Smith constantly keeps you (and him?) guessing. Before you can process the meaning of one image, we're off to another one. Smith seems to keep the viewer distanced and confused consciously. That Smith once said his dreams determined the film's direction makes sense. Smith slept in the studio where he spent a year filming. He'd nap for a bit, then animate whatever dreams he recalled. How truthful this is is questionable. It's more like a combination of being influenced by dreams, the subconscious and the figures he'd already cut out. Ultimately, Smith tried using the intuitive approach to let chance and randomness guide him. How effective that is is questionable. Decisions were made about what to cut and keep, where to place something, and what materials to use. And based on what Smith relays in an interview with

P. Adams Sitney, it's clear that he was making the decision and not leaving it all to chance.

> First, I collected the pieces from old catalogues and books and whatever, then made up file cards of all possible combinations of them; then, I spent maybe a few months trying to sort the cards into logical order. A script was made for that. All the script and the pieces were made for a film at least four times as long. There were wonderful masks and things cut out. Like when the dog pushes the scene away at the end of the film, instead of the title "end" what is really there is a transparent screen that has a candle burning behind it on which a cat fight begins—shadow forms of cats begin fighting. Then, all sorts of complicated effects; I had held these off. It was to be in four parts. It was exhaustingly long in its original form. The cutting that was done was really a correction of timing. It's better in its original form.[6]

Trying to seek the truth in Smith's films is pointless. As Jamie Sexton notes, "Smith has constantly played games with interviewers, mixing imagination and memory when recounting his past."[7] There's something both terrifying and liberating in that concept. Smith (much like the collage animation works of Larry Jordan and others) provides viewers with the freedom to come up with their meanings. There is no single truth, narrative, or theme to be uncovered in Smith's work. This isn't a Hollywood studio movie where you check your head in at the door. After all, you don't need to think because everything is laid out nicely and tidily. When you leave the cinema, that's it, that's all. Smith's collages (like those, as we shall see of Larry Jordan and Lewis Klahr) are complex. He lures you into the idea that a narrative will unfold before taking you somewhere entirely unexpected. This pattern spreads throughout *No. 12*.

As far as we know, *No. 12* would be the last collage animation film Smith would undertake. He worked on a few more film pieces before moving on to other things. Despite only making a handful of collage animations (not to forget his cameraless works before that), Smith's contribution to collage animation and animation, in general, is notable for his remarkable imagery and process and for carrying forward elements of mysticism, surrealism, alchemy, and Dada into animation.

STAN VANDERBEEK (U.S.A.)

The collage animations of Stan VanDerBeek are almost the polar opposite of the occult nature of Harry Smith's mystical works. While Smith went inside for meaning, VanDerBeek openly explored the barrage of images and sounds increasingly saturating and bombarding modern society. He took shots at everything: politicians, technology, sexism, masculinity, consumerism, and even death. All with a wicked sense of humour. Fusing surrealism and pop art, VanDerBeek's rapid-fire collages took the technique in a new and fresh direction that mirrored a fragmented time, one that continues to influence artists from Terry Gilliam to Martha Colburn and Winston Hacking. VanDerBeek's collision of styles and material anticipated the mashed-up videos one encounters on YouTube and assorted social media channels.

VanDerBeek was a self-taught filmmaker. He learned to make films by painting backgrounds for a CBS (Columbia Broadcasting System) kid's show, *Windy Dink and You* (1953–1957). After hours, he'd stay at the studio and then use the studio's animation stand and editing table to make his films.

Before he moved on to computer animation and expanded cinema, VanDerBeek made several collage animations in the 1950s and early 1960s, primarily using cut-out images from magazines, newspapers, advertisements, and even newsreels (in his live-action collage work). VanDerBeek's frantic and sloppy films mirror the anxiety, chaos, and uncertainty of the cold war era, and the increased influence of television and mass media.

Pinning down just when VanDerBeek made a specific film is a challenge. Easily bored, he often worked on multiple movies at once, which explains the presence of recurring images and themes. The rapidity of his output also prioritizes surface images over deeper meanings. Each film feels more like a chapter in a larger story, or as one critic aptly noted: "The cumulative effect is one of radical discontinuity, akin to the experience of flipping through the channels on a television, only to be faced with the realization that each one offers a variation on the same theme."[8] Whatever the results, VanDerBeek's films were rarely dull.

What Who How (1957) is one of his first works that establish several images that would repeat in future works (e.g. hammers, forks and themes of mortality, identity, technological progress, and war). Using an assortment of found photo fragments, VanDerBeek's films tackle a common theme: a society overwhelmed by STUFF. What do we do without material stuff? Who are without new purchases? How do we live without consumer goods? We see a woman's head open, and all these goods emerge; a bug crawls out of a man's mouth. With machine gun delivery, VanDerBeek touches upon themes of consumerism, gender roles, and identity. Just who are we in a world where we are increasingly being sensory assaulted?

In *The Immaculate Contraption or Wheeeels or America on Wheels, Part 1* (1958) and *Wheeeels No. 2* (1959), VanDerBeek turns his satirical eye toward all things car-related, exploring our increasing reliance on motorized vehicles, how the landscape has changed as it accommodates roads and highways, but also motion in general. Gone are the days when people moved naturally, on foot. The car has altered landscapes and rhythms, speeding everything up. Everyone is increasingly in a hurry to nowhere.

With *A La Mode* (1958), VanDerBeek turns his eye toward fashion and precisely how women's roles and identities are shaped by style and make-up industries. Throughout his films, VanDerBeek also takes pokes at men and masculinity. In one of his masterworks, *Science Friction* (1959), the space race is mocked, along with notions of progress and men always wanting more. VanDerBeek uses images of rockets, westerns, TV, guns, and ads to ridicule our constant need to move forward and up. The restlessness one experiences watching VanDerBeek's films is the restlessness of a society chasing its tail. We can – and sometimes should – sit and be quiet, but we've been seduced into constantly moving about. Those in power crave a community that is restless and distracted. A contemplative individual is the last thing needed in that world. Although not technically animated, *Newsreel of Dreams* (1964) is a beautiful summary of this existential restlessness. Using a montage of newsreels, television images, and sounds, VanDerBeek anticipates the era of channel surfing. He shows us a world where it's like you've fallen asleep with the TV still on. Those images and sounds mix and mingle and hijack your dreams and half-awake imaginings. Individual memory becomes uncertain. What did we experience vs what is projected onto us/into us?

> We are beyond decisions … particular acts of seeing, hearing, belief acts of communication, radio, television, telephone have committed our consciousness to another state that is well beyond decisions of consciousness (awareness). Instinct takes over … (driving a car is a perfect example …) the industrial metaphysical revolution has only just begun. This lack of decision however invades our anxiety. Anxiety becomes a motor response, almost another sense (or at least a sense extension).[9]

In *Achooo Mr. Kerroschev* (1959) and *Skullduggery Pt. 2* (1961), those very leaders become the object of VanDerBeek's ridicule as politicians, and various figures are portrayed as cowards, bullies full of hot air. Unfortunately, there's an immaturity here, especially in the *Achoo* film, which features leaders having their bums appear or putting them in drag (which comes across, at least today, as somehow mocking women's fashion, crossdressing, etc.). My point is that it's pretty unlikely these works would affect any meaningful change. Then again, VanDerBeek was fully aware of the limitations of art. "Movies are nothing." he wrote in one interview. "We got to a museum and spend as much time as possible looking at any pretty girl rather than the pictures …"[10]

Breathdeath (1963) is VanDerBeek's most impressive collage work. Incorporating live-action footage, collage, and negative imagery, *Breathdeath* explores gender, identity, illusion, and the utter surrealism of existence. Along the way, he seems to mock mortality. Like, come and get us. We're going to party, dance, and move until we can't.

Collage in VanDerBeek's hands mirrors an out-of-control world that is fragmented, fearful, and losing a sense of self and purpose. Interestingly, VanDerBeek is not anti-technology. What concerned him was a society overwhelmed by the pace of technological change. As he wrote in a 1966 issue of *Film Culture*:

> We must quickly find some way for the entire level of world human understanding to rise to a new human scale. This scale is the world. The risks are the life and death of this world. The technological explosion of this last half century and the implied future are overwhelming; man is running the machines of his invention, while the device that is running man runs the risk of running wild. Technological research, development and involvement of the world community has almost completely outdistanced the emotional-sociological (socio- "logical") comprehension of this technology .... It is this danger ... that man does not have time to talk to himself.. that man does not have means to talk to other men ... the world hangs by a thread of verbs and nouns. Language and cultural semantics are as explosive as nuclear energy.[11]

Much like Terry Gilliam's bits and pieces for Monty Python, VanDerBeek's work is best savoured as a whole. While *Science Friction* and *Breathdeath* are standouts, they are like chapters in a much richer and fuller story that amplifies the power and potency of VanDerBeek's work.

JAN LENICA AND WALERIAN BOROWCZYK (POLAND)

Polish animators Jan Lenica and Walerian Borowczyk (Boro) worked with collage elements together (*Once Upon a Time*, 1957 and *Dom, 1959*) and apart. Now, neither artist was involved deeply with collage. Lenica certainly worked with cut-outs and drawings, often with collage elements, throughout his career as an animator and graphic artist. Still, he only made a few films that fit my reductive-for-the-sake-of-sanity criteria for this particular paper house of words.

The two started collaborating in 1956, and as one critic, the late Marcin Giżycki, noted, there were two eras in Polish animation: before and after Lenica and Boro.[12] Before their emergence, Polish animation was unremarkable and primarily made for younger audiences. The arrival of Lenica and Boro instantly elevated animation to an art form that had more in common with absurd humour and surrealism than with any form of animation.

What was striking about their films (together and apart) was their simplicity and lo-fi, D.I.Y. (Do-It-Yourself) style. They utilized whatever materials they could find: paper, old photographs, cut-out illustrations, and objects. Collage and cut-out materials perfectly suit their absurdist and surrealist tendencies that echo the worlds of Eugene Ionesco (a favourite writer of Lenica) and Kafka. This is not to say that their films were light-hearted comedies. They depicted the chaos of the post-WWII world struggling to find its way back to some semblance of normalcy and decency, a task so overwhelming that all you can do is laugh at the absurdity of the whole existential mess.

Their debut film, *Once Upon a Time* (1957), is remarkably effective despite its simplistic, low-tech nature. The scribbled opening credits and jaunty score make you think this is just another kid's cartoon, one that kids might even make. Then we meet an odd oval cut-out figure that starts walking to the accompaniment of an organ soundtrack. The figure, who can shapeshift, walks around the frame and encounters an assortment of odd figures (angels, animals, statues, phonographs) made from newspaper, film footage, and photo clippings. Eventually, the figure takes shelter in an abstract painting.

Once Upon a Time feels like a freewheeling improv session that celebrates expression in all its awkward and sloppy forms while rejecting and mocking high art (in one scene, a paper hat replaces the bourgeois bowler hat on a character). In a 1957 interview, the duo discussed their aims: "Our ambition is to give a serious meaning to animated film. (...) We don't want to limit ourselves to one stylistic genre, but would prefer to try anything that awakens the imagination, moves people, makes them laugh, gives pleasure to the eye."[13]

Their third and final film together, *House* (1958), takes us inside an apartment building where we briefly encounter a woman. From there, the scenes skirt between a shot of the woman and an assortment of surreal collage scenes composed of assorted cut-out images and illustrations (including footage of two macho athletes – cut-out photos by Étienne Jules Marey – battling each other). Another section uses an assemblage of fruit, hair, and other objects to depict, you guessed it, a wig taking a drink of milk. In another sequence, a man hangs his hat on a hook repeatedly (is this the woman's husband? Is he always coming and going, too preoccupied to give her any attention?). This cycle drifts into a montage of postcards and photo fragments mixed with live-action and coloured cut-out illustrations. Finally, we see the woman making out with the head of a male mannequin before it decays and falls apart.

What does it all mean? Is this a parody of Hollywood melodramas? The abandoned housewife? Are these scenes she's observing in the house? Is she dreaming? Are we inside a troubled woman's mind where we see barely comprehensible fragments that might be memories, hallucinations, or both?

While Lenica remained in Poland, Boro headed off to France. He made his next film, *The Astronauts* (1959), in collaboration with Chris Marker (although it seems Marker's involvement was limited to using his name to secure funding). This satirical sci-fi film tells the story of an astronaut wannabe who travels the galaxy in a homemade spaceship (made up of old newspapers and cardboard) with his owl sidekick. During his "adventures," he flies around town peeking at an unsuspecting young woman, disrupts a parade for some bourgeois guy by blowing his hat off, and tours around the earth a bit before heading into space and eventually crash-landing back home.

With a nod to George Melies' fantastically mixed-media silent films, Boro incorporates photo fragments of urban environments and architecture, pixelation, cut-out photos, newspaper fragments, 19th-century illustrations, postcards, and an assortment of found objects. At once an absurdist parody of science fiction films, *The Astronauts* also gently mocks (like Vanderbeek's *Science Friction*) human obsession with space travel. The film is also unique because it's one of the first collage-inspired works to attempt a somewhat linear narrative.

Grandma's Encyclopedia (1963) is a collection of travel scenarios. The first segment uses assorted etchings and illustration cut-outs while following an absurd automobile race across varied inner and outer landscapes. In the 2nd scenario, similar cut-out illustrations are used for an air race of some sort. The next scene follows a train as it travels across tunnels and landscapes. Like *The Astronauts*, *Grandma's Encyclopedia* is a silly, absurdist work that satirizes transportation (cars, airships, trains). Modern viewers will instantly think of Terry Gilliam's later cut-out animation for Monty Python.

Grandma's Encyclopedia would be Boro's last full-on collage film. *Renaissance* (1963) falls closer into the assemblage category (though an argument can be made that it remains collage), using an assortment of three-dimensional found objects that anticipate the works of The Brothers Quay and Jan Svankmajer. Soon enough, Boro would leave animation behind and turn his attention towards often controversial live-action features that some conservative types denounced as pornographic.

Jan Lenica's films never really veer too profoundly into collage territory. His works tend to combine collage elements with original cut-out figures. *Labyrinth* (1962) is the closest to a full-out collage film. A winged man (made of cut-out illustrations) flies to a city. Now wingless, the man explores the modern city's labyrinth (which is composed of assorted Art Nouveau imagery) in search of something. The town is filled with beasts (dinosaurs, dragonflies, various hybrid human-bird creatures) and unwelcoming sites. Lenica, with elements of deadpan humour, creates an anti-utopia. Underneath its surface beauty, the city is a horror scape of violence, alienation, and deception. In the end, the man grabs his wings and hightails it out of the town, but before he can escape, he is chased by a gaggle of menacing birdmen who devour him.

Like much of Lenica's work, *Labyrinth* is rooted in the Theatre of the Absurd. Combining elements of Buster Keaton, Franz Kafka and Eugene Ionesco, Lenica constructs a partially autobiographical world that addresses the struggle of individuals to find themselves in an increasingly detached and dehumanized society. While Lenica's work is based on the travails of post-WWII Poland, his films expand further and reflect the growing tensions between humanity and technological progress. His inspired combination of cut-out and collage elements neatly mirrors the fragmented nature of his character and their environments. His protagonists trek through violence, paranoia, anxiety, and absurdity. They do not know how to, nor are they sure they want to, fit into an increasingly discombobulated society. Oppression greets them in many forms: paranoia (*Rhinoceros*), language (*A*), exile (*Labyrinth*), humans (*Adam 2*), and even themselves. Each character tries to define and establish a unique blip on life's map.

PITSTOP – ZAGREB FILM

Zagreb Film was famous for its vibrant and layered designs, so it's not entirely surprising that a few of their early films already incorporated elements of collage art. Though there are no full-out collage animation films, Vatroslav Mimica and Vlado Kristl, particularly, were making films that combined cut-out drawings with cut-and-paste elements.

Vatroslav Mimica

The Lonely (1958)

This Kafkaesque tale about a lonely worker without much of a life is primarily a drawn and cut-out film, but collage elements are used in the backgrounds and some objects (i.e. the office desks). Let's say it's collage-y.

At the Photographer's (1959)

A deadpan Buster Keaton-type character wanders through a gallery of bizarre, distorted and occasionally grotesque smiles (stolen from an assortment of magazines). He eventually sits for a photograph. The photographer then struggles to get a smile out of the poor guy. The collage use is readily visible here, mainly through cut-out photographs of assorted faces, mouths, and eyes. Again, collage is more of a secondary player used to complement and enhance the film's original cut-out drawings and absurdist tones.

The Inspector Is Back! (1959)

A police inspector roams the dark city streets in pursuit of a criminal who is only known via his fingerprint. This time, collage elements (primarily photos and newspaper cut-outs) create the city landscape and the inspector's body. In fact, only the inspector's head and feet seem to come from original drawings. The rest of the film is almost entirely composed of collage materials. The use of photo materials gives the film a fragmented, mysterious vibe while adding elements of humour (e.g. as the inspector reads the newspapers, an assortment of images taken from film noirs and other movies are shown). Collage creates a strikingly discombobulated, surrealist (particularly the strange scene where the inspector encounters cut-and-paste photos of women's eyes) and expressionist atmosphere.

Everyday Chronicle (1962)

Hurray, it's another film about the bland, dehumanized workers mechanically walking through a decaying urban setting. The use of collage elements (pictures of food, tools, streetlights, and newspaper fragments) is inspired (notably the cars made from machine parts) and adds a striking contrast to the drabby, flatness of the characters.

Mimica's use of collage is innovative and harkens back to the origins of collage in the way it fuses graphic art and pop culture and hides existentialist-driven stories within a "cartoon" surface. Mimica also uses collage in a more restrained manner. These aren't aggressive improvised sensory explosions, ala VanDerBeek. Mimica uses collage to enhance his narratives. Collage might be a secondary character, but each film would be much more conventional and bland without it.

A brief mention should also be made of Vlado Kristl, who also tinkered with collage elements. La Peau de Chagrin (1960), based on a Honoré de Balzac story, uses newspaper fragments primarily as background material and even constructs a sofa entirely out of newspaper. In his widely acclaimed Don Quixote (1961), Kristl incorporates landscape photos, magazine cut-outs, and newspaper clippings towards the end of the primarily drawn film.

JEANINE & CHRISTIANNE CLERFEUILLE (FRANCE)

Now I am not going to dive into every single animator who dabbled with collage, but there are some worthy of mention here, like the Clerfeuille sisters. I owe my colleague at CNC (Centre national du cinéma et de l'image animée), Jean-Baptiste Garnero, for this late discovery. Biological and artistic twins, the Clerfeuille sisters, were a rarity in a field until much later in the 20th century, almost exclusively dominated by male directors. Among their works were some collage advertising films the duo made in the 1960s. There's nothing too deep about them. They are just beautiful and fun examples of collage that show how it was so quickly adopted for marketing and advertising purposes. Although the Clerfeuille sisters were involved in many productions, only a few are available for viewing.

Le Parisien – Concourt (1960)

One of many advertisements the Clerfeuille sisters created, this one is promoting a contest in the Le Parisien newspaper. A truck appears and unloads a pile of household objects (all represented by cut-out photos). A man collects the things and slowly moves the furniture in an imaginary home in the middle of a field. Once he's created his ideal interior, he sits down and opens a copy of Le Parisien, and a narrator tells us about a contest.

It's a short, funny, and inventive use of collage materials that combines surrealism and absurdity to promote consumerism and material goods. By the 1960s (and likely earlier), collage animation had shifted from its experimental domain towards the advertising world.

Eau Chaude 61 (1961)

Made to promote Gaz/Electricity company, this spot uses cut-out photos of assorted people and objects mixed with some drawn sequences to create another silly and surreal piece of advertising.

1880 (1963, Directed by Jeanine Clerfeuille)

Before AI-generated images or speed and colour-corrected old films, Jeaninine Clerfeuille made this oddly engaging collage animation that attempts to transport viewers to 1880 Paris. Using very basic and straightforward cut-outs of vintage photographs of men, women, horses, and various aspects of 19th-century Paris, *1880* is a strange mix of natural and surreal, a sometimes silly but constantly engaging imagining of what life might once have been like at that time. From daily urban life, the film moves to varied activities like skating, tennis, sailing, running, and car races. The facial and physical movements of the characters are stilted, rudimentary, and quite funny. The combination of the absurdist bits of humour with an operatic soundtrack (especially the scenes where the characters awkwardly mouth the words of the opera) undoubtedly elevates what might have otherwise been a rather dull documentary into an enjoyable piece of historical silliness.

GYÖRGY KOVÁSZNAI AND DEZSÔ KORNISS (HUNGARY)

While Hungarian animation tends to be known for its vibrant, surreal graphic style, some animators were diving into collage animation in the early 1960s, notably the acclaimed artist/painter György Kovásznai and Dezsô Korniss.[14]

Hungarian animation, at this point, was primarily just drawn films made for kids. In 1961, Kovásznai began working with animation at Hungary's state film studio, Pannonia. For the first couple of years, Kovásznai toiled away as a scriptwriter on various short animation and live-action feature films before making his films. Between 1962 and 1983, Kovásznai made 25 animation films, but our focus is on a trio of collage animation short films he made in collaboration with Dezsô Korniss between 1963 and 1969.

Collage animation was not done in Hungary before Kovásznai and Korniss's *Monologue* (1963). Korniss was a key figure connecting the younger generation of the 1950s and 1960s with avant-garde art (including Russian montage) of the early 20th century. The use of collage was an ideal bridge to connect these different eras. While collage had its roots in Dada, Cubism, Surrealism, etc., Kovásznai and Korniss's films show the apparent influence of Lenica, Borowcyzk, and VanDerBeek. The duo used collage to comment on Hungary's past and present, critiquing previous generations while exploring contemporary issues (e.g. gender, sexism) with often biting wit.

Monologue (1963)

The voice in *Monologue* comes from a young woman who reminisces about her grandparent's and parent's past. With the young woman's innocent-sounding voice and the hypnotic sounds of a music box, the viewer is lured into thinking this might be some innocent and nostalgic charmfest very quickly though we see that there's something a bit darker at play here.

The young narrator says:

> The memory of my grandparents is like two colourful shadows or the obsessive, recurring tune of a chiming clock. As tormented as they were throughout their lives
>
> by worries about how to tell the decent from the indecent apart, they lied to each other and deceived themselves.[15]

Monologue is a bold calling out of previous generations for their responsibilities during eras that led to two global wars, and the subsequent rise of psychology, advertising, and quick-fix chemical solutions (not at all like our world today, right?):

> ... the number of psychologists were increasing, many of them becoming famous advertising managers, and giant serpents were writhing in the subconscious,
>
> the seduced crowds almost developed a migraine, but quickly took some Bayer aspirin.[16]

It's a biting assault on past generations for their roles in allowing themselves to be deceived and manipulated and the effect that has had on the past and present. It's as if the young girl is also trying to conquer her torments so that she can move forward with a clear head and heart.

> My first experiences were so bad that it could have been hardly surprising if all good faith and honesty had died out in me for the rest of my life, it is most characteristic of me that I'm much more cautious and careful about illusions than the ancients were. With keen eyes and clear mind, I'm trying to assess the vistas opening up in the new world. I am a child of the age that defies blind destiny, though dim memories still haunt me at times, no, but no! One day they will vanish, like superstitions.[17]

I know we're here to talk about collage, but that is some beautifully blunt writing, a bold interrogation in a society ripe with censorship and government oppression. Animation was supposed to be a diversion for kids, not a critique of culture and politics.

The use of collage provides an excellent cloaking device. Mixing materials from different eras made the film somewhat indecipherable to censors (reminiscent of the way Estonian animators, for example, would use absurdist humour to fool Soviet censors). Fusing surrealism and absurdity provides a cover. No one can be certain what the message of the film is about. Still, the film was so problematic that the head of Hungarian film wanted to ban it immediately, but he was talked out of it by the Pannonia animation studio director.

Collage also appealed to Korniss and Kovásznai for its abstract potential and ability to address contemporary social issues. Collage gave the films life, or rather, they created the sense that the real world was part of the film. As Brigitta Iványi-Bitter writes: "The inner microcosm of the 'collage films' – always meant a 'live film'; breathing life that had to be suggested instead of being filmed: to be suggested, being delved into the chaos of contradictions and discouraging failures, … intoxicated with sweet and ruthless, depressing yet exciting, unfathomable yet comprehensible life."

The collage materials include vintage illustrations, print ads, photos, illustrations of angels, nurses, Fred Astaire, dancing women, and a big-headed guy with a moustache (all men of power?). The use of contemporary and often recognizable collage imagery also gave the film a universal doorway to viewers. "Richard Avedon's photo and Audrey Hepburn's attire demonstrate a close relationship between certain frames of *Monologue* and the most fashionable photo art of the era."[18]

The young woman could be from anywhere. Even a Canadian, American, or German would make connections. The voice of *Monologue* is a voice of the time, of the generation. Even if one couldn't speak Hungarian, a gateway toward comprehension can be located via recognizable photo imagery.

Young Man Playing the Guitar at the Old Master's Gallery (1964)

Made as a sequel to *Monologue*, *Young Man Playing the Guitar at the Old Master's Gallery* is a bit of sex, abstract painting and rock and roll. The central images include a nude woman and a tiny young man strumming his guitar to contemporary pop music. Between them, an assortment of abstract paintings appears in the background.

On the surface, it's not a film that stands out as anything remarkable, let alone controversial, yet it was banned in June 1965, right after its premiere.

Because state censors had already had their eye on *Monologue*, *Young Man* was immediately treated with suspicion. It's really hard to fathom just what it was that triggered the banishment. Did censors see it as an erotic fantasy (there is some occasional moaning)? A young man "getting off" to images or thoughts of a nude woman? Was it the use of rock music (associated with those monstrously indecent capitalist youth from the West)? Perhaps it was an issue with the young man, who went against the "pragmatic, rational, goal-oriented socialist male ideal."[19] Let's face it: The guy is petite, boyish, and immature when placed alongside the more prominent, more restrained nude woman. He's behaving like, well, a typical hormone-raging teen (that said, at the end of the film, the man is joined by a woman of the same size to pull down the end credit).

Best that you seek the film and decide for yourselves. That said, it's a minor film in some ways, and if it hadn't been banned, it might have drifted quietly and rapidly into history's rearview mirror.

The Cricket's Wedding/Pastoral Dance (1969)

This film is a bit of an oddball. It's not animated, and there certainly isn't any linear narrative. It's more of a live-action montage with many zooms and abrupt cuts. Armed with a few vintage photos and some cut-outs of characters in folk costumes, it is a collage of pre-existing paintings that serve as a rapid history of Hungarian art from 19th-century realism to 1960s abstraction. In a sense, it's a work that links folk and high art (via montage/collage techniques) to connect past Hungarian life with the contemporary one. And hey, isn't that how we got started with this whole collage story? You can't have a present without the past.

Rather than having me cook up some half-assed analysis based on the little that I know about Hungarian society in the 1960s, let's turn to my colleague Brigitta Iványi-Bitter to get a better sense of what she thinks made these few collage films so vital:

> So the three pillars of their work: bridging old and new artistic styles through new technology; inventing new ways of filmmaking; co-operation with older generations and especially collage based on photography, the single greatest technological invention that created the image revolution by the early 20th century, and it was the disassembling of photography in collages which showed the kind of disappointment and fear of the wartimes through collage artworks in the 1920s and 1930s in Paris. And this had a great impact on all Central European artists by the end of the 1930s, and they carried it with them through their collage animations over the other side of the iron curtain.[20]

PITSTOP: TODOR DINOV, IVAN ANDONOV AND BULGARIAN ANIMATION

The use of collage elements also found its way into Bulgarian animation. While Jan Lenica and the Zagreb studio were apparent influences, inspiration came from another source: poster art. "The attitude towards the modernistic image, both for artists in animation and for the whole cultural community in Bulgaria, was the Exhibition of Polish Posters at the end of 1954 in Sofia," notes Velislava Gospondinova in her writing on cut-out and collage use in Bulgarian animation. "Most of the events that shaped the idea of the modern flat image and collage principle in Bulgarian animation were poster exhibitions."[21]

Collage elements began appearing in the 1960s in Bulgarian animation. *Pictures from An Exhibition* (Hristo Topunzanov, 1963) mixes puppets with sprinkles of objects and cut-outs from old photos and illustrations. *Jealousy* (Todor Dinov, 1963) uses a mix of drawings and photo cut-outs of flowers, guitars, guns, and other objects alongside minimalist drawings in this somewhat silly story about a musical note that comes to life and becomes entangled in a love triangle/Western. *Birds* (Ivan Andonov, 1966) combines cut-out materials of birds (the birds appeared to be constructed by cut-out images of seeds) with what seems to be photo cut-outs of feathers and flowers.

Gospodinova suggests the link via poster art led many Bulgarian animators to discover Cubism, Dada, and Constructivism:

> The use of photography in a collage-montage-constructed composition was highlighted in poster and graphic design exhibitions from France, Germany (West and East), Switzerland, Poland, Czechoslovakia, and Hungary. Reviews of them show that, despite detours and the use of politically correct rhetoric at the time, such modernist aesthetics began to not only enter the Bulgarian cultural space, but also to slowly establish themselves among the art circles.[22]

While most of the Bulgarian animation films of this period utilize collage elements in the background, the most exciting pieces that come closest to collage animation come from Todor Dinov and Ivan Andonov.

Banished from Eden (Todor Dinov, 1967) a jazzy piece about a musician who dies and heads for heaven (momentarily). *Banished from Eden* combines live-action footage, photo montages, and collage elements (photo, religious iconography, venus de milo, and various artworks). The mixed media approach, reminiscent of the Zagreb studio animators, creates a vibrant work that, like so many films of the time, deals with an individual finding their way in a somewhat confusing landscape.

A Difficulty (Ivan Andonov, 1967) is a lighthearted tale featuring a cut-out character making his way through a maze constructed from collage materials (fabrics, illustrations, photos, texts from books, etc.) An allegory about the labyrinth that is life, the use of collage materials creates a work that teeters Klahbetween realism and surrealism.

Esperanza (Ivan Andonov, 1967) is closest to a full-on collage animation work that we get in Bulgarian animation of this period. This complex,
multi-layer work combines live-action footage, archival footage, and photos
(fittingly, one of Picasso appears briefly), with an assortment of found objects
(dishes, guitars) and magazine photo advertisements (cars, domestic spaces).
The result is a richly inventive modernist work that has more in common with
VanDerBeekand Keen than any other Bulgarian animation of the period.

LARRY JORDAN (U.S.A.)

If there were an award for longest serving collage animator or most dedicated,
it would undoubtedly be American Larry Jordan. Since the 1950s, Jordan has
made over 80 films, with at least 60 animated collage works. Influenced by
Max Ernst and Joseph Cornell, Jordan's collage works primarily use 19th-
century engravings and illustrations that give his films a mystical, otherworldly vibe. His collage landscapes (resembling Harry Smith's alchemic
roots) are akin to drifting through the bardo, a state of existence between
death and rebirth (think George Saunders' novel *Lincoln in the Bardo*, which
takes place in that same realm). Jordan describes his films as taking place in
a "limbo world … it's not Paradiso and it's not Pugatorio."[23]

Jordan's films are essentially an unloading of subconscious materials that even he's sometimes trying to figure out what the finished work
means. "I often operate on freely associated series of images," says Jordan.
"Finding the trail as I go, not plotting it, though some of the films are metic-
ulously scripted. When I astonish myself, I put it in the film. When I don't,
I leave it out." [24]

Larry Jordan began making films (primarily experimental, live-action
shorts) in the early 1950s. While studying at Harvard, he took an interest
in the films of Sergei Eisenstein and experimental cinema. With his pal,
Stan Brakhage, he made several live-action, experimental films. In the mid-
1950s, now living in New York, Jordan discovered the work of more experimental artists, including Joseph Cornell (who would significantly influence
his art).

In the late 1950s, the artist Jess introduced Jordan to the collage novels
of Max Ernst. These works inspired Jordan to begin making collages from
cut-out engravings and soon led to cinematic experiments with animated collage. Animation had long attracted and repulsed Jordan: "The technique of
animation is natural to me, and has its basis in the love-hate relationship I had
with the cartoons and comedies in the magic ritual of childhood."[25]

The idea to make collages move all happened, fittingly, during an afternoon nap. "In 1961, when I woke up from a nap, I had the realization that I could make engravings move since I knew the essentials of animation."[26]

For Jordan, working with cut-out materials was a joy from the start: "Working with cut outs allows me to achieve a movement that is partly natural and partly completely artificial—a strangeness I find very appealing. Also, engraved and printed material is very photogenic."[27]

One of Jordan's initial forays into animation is an anomaly in his filmography. *Swine* (1963) is a cross between VanDerBeek and Dada, a rapid montage of photos, cut-out texts, film footage, music sheets, hair brushes, and a fire hose all grooving about to The Beatles': "I Saw Her Standing There."

Other early animation works include *The Soccer Game* (1959), *Minerva Looks Out into the Zodiac* (1959), and *The Dream Merchant* (1964), but it's really with *Duo Concertantes* (1964) that we start to get the whole experience of Jordan's collage animation.

The uniqueness of Jordan's collage work is that he creates this unified world that gives the illusion of narrative and wholeness. There's no mix of cut-outs, drawings, live-action, etc. The backgrounds and assorted characters are all composed of cut-out illustrations. It provides an illusion of comfort and stability for the viewer as they start upon a wild, surreal ride.

Now, Jordan's oeuvre is worth a book all its own. It is so rich, diverse, and thoughtful that no one can do justice to its splendours in a book like this, so let's do our best to hike, stumble, and bumble through a few personal highlights of his extraordinary animated collages.

Duo Concertantes (1964)

This black-and-white collage work was the first of Jordan's animated films to garner attention. The familiar flashing orb that occupies a place in many of his films is already present here. We see theatre performance pamphlets, assorted 19th-century illustrations and figures consisting of hands, human-bird hybrids, butterfly-human hybrids, statues, elephants, dogs, birds, cats, planets, and objects. You feel like you're in the midst of a science experiment. It's a world of whatever, where anything goes, like all of Jordan's collage work to follow, its mystifyingly beautiful. You don't think Jordan's films; you sit back and feel them like you would the warmth of the afternoon sun. There's an aura of tranquility and patience throughout Jordan's work. Most collage animation has a frantic, fragmented and breathless pace, but Jordan's work is decidedly eloquent. None of that rabble-rouser, LSD vibes here; this is a world of exquisite lyricism.

Gymnopédie (1966)

Greeted, again, with a vintage theatre bill, along with the soothing sounds of Erik Satie and a hypnotic blue tint, we are welcomed into a theatre of the unknown. In an old rural landscape, a butterfly lady enters with an assortment of bottles and that familiar orb. As with *Duo Concertantes*, it's a world where characters and objects are freed from the constraints of their original contexts and meanings. Events begin without end. A horse gallops to nowhere, an egg floats through the land and an acrobat swings on a rope in Venice. It's all one big metaphysical playground where we are encouraged to sit back and enjoy the show without worrying about what it's all about, kinda like life. It's a lesson in learning to accept the absurdity of it all, to let go of searching for meaning, for purpose. It all passes by. It's a refreshing contrast to the dark and dour interpretations of the absurd and mortality often seen in art and literature. *Gymnopédies* takes joy in the fleeting, rudderless temporality of life.

Our Lady of the Sphere (1969)

With alternating tints of red, green, and blue, and an assortment of 19th-century paintings, illustrations, engravings, and circus photos along with Jordan's familiar "buzzing" orb visual motif, *Our Lady of the Sphere* follows the journey of a young boy with an orbital head who travels through the Underworld encountering an assortment of odd creatures (a diver, a lady with an orbital head) and landscapes including an apparent carnival (how we try to hide the reality of mortality through distractions?). A scene of horses starting at a painting of a talking pelican is also a particularly memorable comic moment, as is the recurring image of the victorian-era woman wearing an orb for a head. At times you feel you're safely adrift inside a person's subconscious, of all of that person's memories and experiences mixed with snapshots of what was via their ancestors. You are not just you. You are your blood and what bled and breathed before you entered the light.

Once Upon a Time (1974)

A burst of dissolving colours and smoke explodes on the screen before we encounter an assortment of mystical characters, cartoon drawings, drawn animation parts and objects (including the lady with the orb head) accompanied by the voice-over from unseen spirits. This is classic Jordan iconography mixed with a more modern vibe that, in fits, resembles some of the visual elements of the trippy 1970s children's television show, *The Hilarious House of Frightenstein*. *Once Upon a Time* is a gorgeous, creepy, and complex work about spirits and the Underworld. A young man, in this case, seems to be wandering through the afterlife before meeting an orb-head woman who will guide him to another realm.

The Rime of the Ancient Mariner (1977)

Let's make mention of this oddity in Jordan's filmography, a 42-minute work that mixes Samuel Coleridge's epic poem with Gustav Dore's engravings and the narration of Orson Welles. It might be the most accessible or narrative-driven of Jordan's works. As intriguing as the film is, the background story is arguably more riveting.

The story goes that while standing in a bank in San Anselmo, California, Jordan encountered two men looking at a first edition of *The Rime of the Ancient Mariner* with illustrations by Gustav Dore. Viewing the book upside down, Jordan was instantly mesmerized by the engravings inside it. He immediately left the bank and offered to buy the book from the men. They offered it to him for $40 ("about all the money I had in the bank at the time," recalled Jordan). For years and years, he held onto the book, confident that he wanted to do something with it. In terms of reading the poem, the obvious choice was the hefty voice of Orson Welles. Thanks to some connections at the American Film Institute, Jordan managed to get in touch with Welles, who almost immediately agreed (in exchange for 25% of the grant that Jordan would get – largely thanks to Welles' involvement). Using a rough cut from another poem recording, Jordan mapped out a 20-minute film. But, when he got Welles' recording, there was an issue. His reading ran for about 40 minutes. "I was stuck with a forty-minute film which is quite different in animation from a 20-minute film. All the imagery then had to be keyed to the final cutting of his voice."[28]

The end result is a beautiful interpretation that, well, drags a bit after a while.

Sophie's Place (1986)

With little doubt, *Sophie's Place*, a gorgeous, improvised animated collage feature that took five years to finish, is among Jordan's most ambitious projects. An assortment of full-colour characters (including a sad balloon face that floats around under the gaze of a victorian woman), figures and objects interact in this hypnotically magical and cryptic work. While it is loosely based on Sophia, the Greek goddess of wisdom, what it means is up to each of you, the patient, the open-minded viewer. Not even Jordan can tell you what the hell it's all about:

> Full hand-painted cut-out animation. Totally unplanned, unrehearsed development of scenes under the camera, yet with more 'continuity' than any of my previous animations, while meditating on some phase of my life. I call it an alchemical autobiography. The film begins in a paradisia-cal garden. It then proceeds to the interior of the Mosque of St. Sophia. More and more the film develops into episodes centering around one form or another of Sophia, an early Greek and Gnostic embodiment of spiritual wisdom. She is seen emanating light waves and symbolic objects. (But I must emphasize that I do not know the exact significance of any of the symbols in the film any more than I know the meaning of my dreams, nor do I know the meaning of the episodes. I hope that they - the symbols and the episodes - set off poetic associations in the viewer. I mean them to be entirely open to the viewer's own interpretation.)[29]

Jordan's description of the film as a sort of autobiography is misleading. It suggests a narrative and an unearthing of moments from life. Still, the col-lision of assorted shapes, eggs, body parts, and winged creatures leaves you wondering just what kind of autobiography he's on about and what kind of bizarre life the man has led!

But, Jordan calls it an "alchemical autobiography," which suggests some-one roaming through the dustbins of their subconscious – and Jordan's mas-sive collection of materials, whose origins perhaps connect them to specific periods and locations in Jordan's life.

Although Jordan's career has travelled along numerous technological developments and well into the 21st century (he continues to make films in his 88th year of earthly existence), it's surprising that he hasn't experimented with digital technology tools. Working with 16-mm film throughout his career, Jordan has been, on the one hand, reluctant to change everything. "I've slowly acquired a whole working studio of 16mm equipment and I'd have to change everything and that would be too hard and too expensive and too cumber-some."[30] Beyond that, Jordan rightly expresses concerns about using digital and computer animation tools: "The movement comes out of a program, it doesn't come out of the creator. I'm looking for individuality behind the work otherwise it's just the same thing over and over, somebody going through the motions so I don't see anything in digital but then I'm an old fart."[31]

The experience of Larry Jordan's vast, still-rolling and often unappre-ciated (at least within the animation realm) is strangely – and refreshingly – meditative. It's refined chaos. You're sitting in a tea room with a friend and observing that "ah, yes, the world is temporal and has fleeting meaning, if any. We are merely tourists, passersby."

THE BRITISH INVASION – BOB GODFREY, JEFF KEEN AND TERRY GILLIAM

Before he went over to drawn animation, British animator Bob Godfrey dabbled with collage. His early films, *Do It Yourself Animation Kit* (1961) and *The Rise and Fall of Emily Sprod* (1962), influenced by satirical and absurdist comedy like the influential BBC Radio show, *The Goons*, are more linear and narrative-driven than the collage films we've explored. However, he frequently satirizes politics and sexuality. And yet again, for those of us whose introduction to collage and cut-out animation was via Terry Gilliam, we see yet another artist who impacted the Python's member's collage direction. If VanDerBeek and Boro inspired Gilliam from a visual perspective, Godfrey's humour, especially in *Do It Yourself Animation Kit*, clearly influenced Gilliam's deadpan mockery of authority figures.

Do It Yourself Animation Kit features a cut-out character dressed as an army official (again, solid Monty Python vibes) trying to sell a mail-order animation kit so you can make your films at home. Godfrey uses cuts out from newspapers, illustrations, advertisements, currency, appropriated cartoon characters, and landscapes. It's a ridiculous film that, along the way, parodies the tedious process of animation creation. It's no collage classic, but it is an example of collage being used for more comedic, mainstream purposes.

Godfrey followed that up with *The Rise and Fall of Emily Sprod*, a comic tale about a woman trying to flee an unhappy marriage and empty existence. Godfrey uses a combination of drawings, live-action segments, and collage fragments from assorted vintage and contemporary photos and illustrations. The collision of imagery and sounds, although far less ambitious than Smith, VanDerBeek or Breer, nevertheless disrupts the narrative. As nonsensical as the film is, themes of alienation and disconnect lurk behind the madness.

Two off The Cuff (1969) is a drawn film with collage elements that explores individual unhappiness in an increasingly fractured society. The collage portions (not animated) appear in the somewhat dated and sexist fantasy segments of the clown protagonist (who eventually gets his comeuppance).

Henry 9 till 5 (1970) mixes draws and collage elements (photos, sex magazines, nude photos, silent movie footage, newspaper clippings) to tell a comic Kafkaesque story about a sex-obsessed and very bland office employee.

JEFF KEEN

A lesser-known collage animation contributor is Jeff Keen. Although Keen was more in the realm of live-action cinema and painting, he also created some mesmerizing collage animation works that make him worthy of mention. Even in his strictly live-action, experimental works, compositing and montage or collage elements are at play. "In Keen's films, innovative techniques of film construction and transmission – collage, animation, found footage, hand-altered film stock, multiple screen projections – that sought to expand cinema beyond its conventional limits are explored within the context of a diverse array of influences."[32]

Influenced by Pop Art, Surrealism and Fluxus, Keen's films have a modern and satirical sensibility as he seeks to try to make sense of the chaos of the here and now. Comic books, Hollywood B-movies, and an assortment of pop culture influence his films like Cineblatz and Marvo Movie (from 1967). In a rapid-fire, playful, and defiant manner, Keen's world is one of creation and destruction; he attempts to sort through the chaos of post-war Western society and consumerism.

Instant Cinema (filmed in 1962 with a soundtrack added by Keen in 2007) is a typically frenetic piece filled with drawings, toys, objects, illustrations, and photos. An assault on the senses that mirrors a subconscious that itself is hijacked every moment by mass society.

Flik Flak (1964–1965) is more chill – the soundtrack. A relatively mellow but steady bebop score accompanies a collision of cut-out images taken from 19th-century illustrations, comic books, advertisements, and magazines featuring historical and famous figures along with toy guns and assorted objects that Keen frequently riffs on with coloured markers and circular dots that litter the screen like celebratory zits.

In *Cineblatz*, Keen captures the dizzying sensation of our blistering fast food sensory internet existence in this rapid blip of chaos. Keen, anticipating our social media/internet experience, gives us no escape, no centre to grasp. We are bombarded with a fractured kaleidoscope of broken images that, like junk food, exit as fast as they enter. It all feels so urgent, so essential, yet in the end, there's nothing but a mess of people shaking and cowering in a corner, popping smiley pills in a futile attempt to exterminate the demons of anxiety, fear, emptiness, and confusion, which doesn't exist in the first place. As the old banker from St. Louis, T.S. Eliot, once scribbled, "This is the way world ends/This is the way the world ends/This is the way the world ends/not with a bang but a whimper."[33]

Marvo Movie is hilariously described in the official synopsis: "the waters of the English Channel at Brighton beach and the woodland and tip in the surrounding area meet strange costumed happenings in a domestic apartment." I mean, sure, but what unfolds is a jarring collage of live action, superimposition, and stop motion with a haunting soundtrack of whispering voices to create an utterly mysterious and somewhat unnerving atmosphere. Filmmaker Ken Russell, after seeing the film, said, "It went right over my head and seemed a little threatening, but I'm all for it."[34]

Like the work of Bruce Bickford, every frame of Keen's work feels like it's going to burst about any second (and, of course, it does). Before you can even contemplate one frame, another has taken over: "Nothing stands still in his work; it is a constant process in which images and sounds evolve in quick succession through what Keen called 'violently disconnected and overlapping patterns' of destruction, creation and accumulation."[35]

TERRY GILLIAM[36]

Later in the 1960s, we encounter a person who is arguably the most popular and recognizable collage animator around the globe: Terry Gilliam. Gilliam's absurdist, biting, and rather naughty collages were famously featured as part of the British television series *Monty Python's Flying Circus*.

As a kid watching the show, the animation on *Monty Python's Flying Circus* was the prime attraction, the doorway, since I had no idea what the sketches were about. Gilliams' animations were the first unconventional animation most of my generation saw as kids. The appeal to them was twofold. First, they felt naughty. A secret little world where we could snicker at the world. Secondly, unlike the animation of Disney or whatever we were exposed to on television and in cinemas in the 1970s, Gilliam's animation felt accessible. We could do that. We could cut pictures out and make them do funny things. It was like what we did in school.

On the one hand, Gilliam's cut-out collages were infantile and far removed from the ambitions of VanDerBeek or Jordan. Still, Gilliam's satirical pieces are very much rooted in the mischievous aspects of Dada and absurdism. Gilliam's work criticizes consumerism, authority, religion and, well, just about anything "proper." There's often no deeper intent beyond just embarrassing those concepts, authority figures, and institutions. That's okay. They remain (even if the creator is now a world-famous millionaire) as valid a form of counter-culture as anything Smith or VanDerBeek created. Indeed, for me, as a child, Gilliam's work was an awakening. These cartoons critiqued a world and system I didn't realize we were even allowed to question.

"I got into animation, as with most things in my life, by stumbling backwards," recalls Gilliam. "I knew I always loved animation. I rate *Pinocchio* and *Snow White* as the biggest influences in everything I've done, but I didn't have the patience to be like Disney and his team."

While living in New York, Gilliam used to go on the streets and steal used and often blank film stock. "I would draw on it and do things like that. I would do flipbooks. So I had the basic principles of animation."

His beginnings in animation began in the 1960s in London while working on a TV show, *Have Ways of Making You Laugh*. "I was basically drawing cartoons, caricatures of the guests that came out, and that's what I did. And one week they had literally two months worth of terrible punning connections from a DJ that they didn't know what to do. And I said, well, let me make an animated film of it."

With a budget of 400 pounds and a time frame of two weeks to complete a three-minute film, Gilliam's solution was to use cut-outs:

> I had seen cut-out animation, in New York when I lived there in the early sixties. Stan VanDerBeek, and a couple others that always stuck in my head. There was one, I think it was a VanDerBeek piece where he had a cut-out head of Richard Nixon trying to speak and there was a cut-out foot stuck going in his mouth all the time as his boat putting his foot in his mouth. And that stuck with me. So I thought that's how I could do this. So I got a lot of photographs of the DJ, who I was then gonna animate to cut his mouth out, wiggle it up and down, and do silly things with it, that's all. And it went out on this television show I was on, and I became an animator overnight just like that. I've been cheating my way ever since.

In his memoir, Gilliamesque, Gillam writes about his surprise when he re-watched VanDerBeek's work in later years (notably *Breath Death*) and saw how much he'd been influenced: "Many of my ideas for my later cut-out animations I borrowed (to put it politely) from him - the tops of heads come off, feet go in mouths, it's the same shit, I just (oh, alright then ...) stole it – but not consciously, your honour."[37]

Later, Gilliam joined a show called *Do Not Adjust Your Set* with future Pythons, Michael Palin, Terry Jones, and Eric Idle. "They wanted me to do some animation. So I did a thing called 'The Christmas Card,' in which I collected a bunch of Victorian Christmas cards and violated them in various ways. Very quickly, I was becoming well known because this stuff was going out on television, and there were only three channels in England in those days."

Beware of Elephants (1968–1969)

This stream-of-conscious pre-Python short was made for *Do Not Adjust Your Set*. The black and white collage short begins with an extremely short man (using a photo head and cut-out body parts) who is stomped on (anticipating the Python foot) by an elephant. The man's decapitated head is then found and used as a ball by a collection of footballers (whose heads are from various historical figures). Their heads soon appear under a magnifying glass leading to a laundry detergent commercial. This nonsensical short has all the hallmarks of what Gilliam would explore during his Monty Python years.

Monty python collages

As most anyone knows nowadays, the animation segments were set up to provide space between the comedy sketches. This structure liberated the Pythons from having conventional endings to their segments. They'd simply be interrupted by Gilliam's absurdist animations. It proved effective while adding another level of innovation to the series (and later, the feature films).

Given the ubiquitousness of all things Python, there's no need to dive into the segments in detail. Most readers have long ago memorized some of Gilliam's most memorable pieces: "Killer Cars" (where a mutant cat is called upon to stop homicidal cars), "American Defense Toothpaste Ad," "The Baby stroller" (a baby devours unsuspecting old ladies), "The Prince and the Black Spot," "The Hand" (some call it The Statue, the one where a hand keeps trying to remove a leaf from the private part of Michelangelo's David), "Conrad Poohs and his Dancing Teeth," the opening credits and the legendary foot, etc.

Gilliam spent hours roaming around shops and Libraries (including the Hulton picture library in London) and bringing images to Atlas Photography on Regent Street in London. "I'd go roaring in there at night with old engravings from Dover Art books all earmarked with little markings and dimensions, then they'd blow them up as required for me."[38] Gilliam collected Victorian nudes, photos of soldiers, politicians, and other stuffy-looking dead people, whatever he could alter and mock. For many of the bizarre sounds in his films, Gilliam used the BBC's Sound Effects Library and their 33-rpm records. Of course, he was also helped out by his fellow Pythons, often stopping them in a hallway to record their dialogue.

Much to Gilliam's surprise, the show was a success, but more so the animation segments (obviously, many like-minded kids from my generation were sneaking peeks of the show!). As innovative as the comedy sketches were, Gilliam's collage segments were lauded for their uniqueness and humour. His animation has become so influential (*South Park* is one obvious example) that we tend to forget just how uncommon and groundbreaking Gilliams' work was at the time. There had not been anything like them on Television – or anywhere else (except maybe VanDerBeek films).

The Miracle of Flight (1974)

Unlike most collage animators, Gilliam was focused on the story. "The whole point of animation to me is to tell a story, make a joke, express an idea. The technique itself doesn't really matter. Whatever works is the thing to use."[39] This is consistent throughout Gilliam's animation pieces.

The Miracle of Flight parodies humanity's desire to fly through a series of scenarios (e.g. a man simply waving his arms up and down before tumbling to the ground; constructing a giant metallic bird costume before falling off a cliff; having feathers stuck onto a body before, you guessed it, falling off the edge of a cliff. Let's cut this short: they all fall off the edge of the cliff!). In the film, Gilliam uses his usual assortment of found materials (vintage photos, illustrations, portraits, landscape imagery) that Gilliam cuts and tweaks (his manipulation of old photo portraits and adding bulging eyes or big teeth etc., is a common trait throughout his work) and recontextualizes along with absurd sounds and voice contributions from some of his fellow Pythoners.

Storytime (1979)

Although released in 1979 (likely capitalizing on Gilliam's fame via Monty Python), *Storytime* features three animated segments that were made initially for *Do Not Adjust Your Set* (1968) and *The Marty Feldman Comedy Machine* (1971–1972). In the first story, *Don the Cockroach*, Don the happy cockroach is killed almost immediately by a giant foot. The story follows the man whose foot killed Don, then his brother and on and on it goes until the film returns to the beginning and Don is introduced again. A voice and intertitle interrupt the story and put an end to that segment.

The 2nd segment, "The Albert Einstein Story," follows a man who is not THAT Einstein, but merely a nice guy with good hands, hands that he is nice to and that are nice to him. Unfortunately, one of the hands is cheating with a foot. This causes a great uproar in upper-class hand society.

The final segment, "The Christmas Card" (which opens with drawn animation before shifting to cut-out collages), harkens back to Gilliam's earlier comments on vulgarizing Christmas cards. In this case, Gilliam takes an assortment of 19th-century Christmas cards and creates utterly absurd and violent scenarios from them (e.g. birds and deers being shot, Santa being beamed by snowballs by kids, an avalanche crushing people, Santa being an ass to kids).

Gilliam uses a mixture of victorian, early 20th-century and Hollywood photos, along with assorted body parts and backgrounds. In all of Gilliam's collage animation works, the clash between these often naive or stuffy images and the silly new contexts that Gilliam places them within enhances the comedic and absurdist elements of his work while not-so-subtly taking the piss out of humans and our various customs and behaviours. Gilliams' work peels off the mask of civility to show the dark, naughty, violent, and utterly insane tendencies of humanity.

> In the seventeenth century, Puritan iconoclasts used to painstakingly snip our representations of God or the Holy Spirit (which they consider sinful) in pre-Reformation religious artworks. My approach was a good deal more frivolous. I'd find people in serious situations – soldiers in war-time, politicians on the campaign trail - and liberate them by putting them in a dress and making them do something ridiculous. The more solemn and even humourless the original characters, the more potentially funny they were.[40]

And now for something completely ... similar, Chapter 4.

NOTES

1 Oral history interview with Robert Breer, 1973 July 10. Archives of American Art, Smithsonian Institution.
2 Interview with Robert Breer, Guy L. Coté. *Film Culture*, Issue 27, 1962/63, pp. 17–20.
3 Oral history interview with Robert Breer, 1973 July 10. Archives of American Art, Smithsonian Institution.
4 www.artforum.com/print/197205/animating-the-absolute-harry-smith-36216.
5 https://dreamsbuiltbyhand.blogspot.com/2020/04/harry-smith-11-mirror-animations-1956-57.html.
6 www.artforum.com/print/197205/animating-the-absolute-harry-smith-36216.
7 http://www.sensesofcinema.com/2005/experimental-cinema/harry_smith/.
8 https://www.academia.edu/1024405/Stan_VanDerBeek_From_the_Ivory_Tower_to_the_Control_Room.

9   Stan VanDerBeek, "Interview: Chapter One," *Film Culture* 25, Winter 1964–65, p. 20.

10 Stan VanDerBeek, "Interview: Chapter One," *Film Culture* 25, Winter 1964–65, p. 20.

11 Stan VanDerBeek, "'Culture: Intercom' and Expanded Cinema: A Proposal and Manifesto," *Film Culture* 40, 1966.

12 https://culture.pl/en/artist/walerian-borowczyk.

13 https://culture.pl/en/work/house-walerian-borowczyk-jan-lenica.

14 I am deeply indebted to my colleague Brigitta Ivanyi-Bitter for her help contextualizing Kovásznai's collage animation.

15 Iványi-Bitter, Brigitta. *Kovásznai: A Cold War Artist: Animation, Painting, Freedom.* Budapest: Kovásznai Research Center Foundation, 2016, p. 67.

16 ibid.

17 Ibid.

18 Iványi-Bitter, Brigitta. *Kovásznai: A Cold War Artist: Animation, Painting, Freedom.* Budapest: Kovásznai Research Center Foundation, 2016, p. 68.

19 Iványi-Bitter, Brigitta. *Kovásznai: A Cold War Artist: Animation, Painting, Freedom.* Budapest: Kovásznai Research Center Foundation, 2016, p. 76.

20 Conversation with the author, December 2022.

21 Modernism Beyond the Iron Curtain: Collage and Cut-outs in the 60s Bulgarian Animation through the Prism of Poster Art, Velislava Gospodinova, ASIFA Magazine, 2023.

22 Ibid.

23 *A Line of Sight: American Avant-Garde Film Since 1965* by Paul Arthur, University of Minnesota Press, Minneapolis, 2005, p. 63.

24 https://expcinema.org/site/en/events/beyond-enchantment-films-lawrence-jordan.

25 *Experimental Animation: An Illustrated Anthology* by Robert Russett and Cecile Starr, 1974, p. 155.

26 Email exchange with the author, July 29, 2022.

27 Email exchange with the author, July 29, 2022.

28 Interview with Lawrence Jordan, Patricia Kavanagh. *Animatrix*, Issue 15, 2007, pp. 28–29.

29 http://lawrencecjordan.com/films/sophies_place.php.

30 Interview with Lawrence Jordan, Patricia Kavanagh. *Animatrix*, Issue 15, 2007, p. 33.

31 Ibid.

32 https://www.jeffkeen.co.uk/.

33 From Eliot's 1925 poem, *The Hollow Men*.

34 http://www.screenonline.org.uk/film/id/1348466/index.html.

35 https://www.tate.org.uk/documents/531/jeff_keen_programme_notes_0.pdf.

36 Unless otherwise noted, all of Gilliam's quotes are from a 2021 interview with Jeanette Jeanenne of the GLAS Animation Festival.

37 *Gilliamesque: A Pre-posthumous Memoir.* New York: Harper Design, 2016, p. 78.

38 *Gilliamesque : A Pre-posthumous Memoir.* New York: Harper Design, 2016, p. 145.

39 Quote from Bob Godfrey's 1974 series, *Do It Yourself Animation Show*, which can be found on YouTube.

40 *Gilliamesque: A Pre-posthumous Memoir.* New York: Harper Design, 2016, p. 132.

Hi-Fi Cadets Kidnapping a Jukebox of Frank Pearly Oysters

1970/1980s

4

Hungarian artist Sándor Reisenbüchler never envisioned himself as an animator, let alone one making collage films: "I never wanted to make an animated film in my life. If I ever dreamed of making a film, I wanted to make films like the late Zoltán Huszárik made. His poetic short films could not be categorised in any kind of way. He was too poetic for a documentary filmmaker, but documentary enough for film poetry. For me, his world was the most attractive."[1]

Unfortunately, a lung infection that Reisenbüchler contracted as a kid made it difficult for him to work outdoors, so he walked away from documentaries and turned to animation. Two of the biggest influences on Reisenbüchler's work were Jan Lenica and Walerian Borowczyk:

> I had two role models. I thought they were the greatest in Eastern Europe and I said to myself that I had to reach one of their levels. I watched Lenica's *Monsieur Tete* at least 20 times, but I also watched almost everything by Borowczyk, who also made animated films early in his career. At that time, these films were shown in film clubs, and I always sat in to watch the Poles. I was very fond of them.[2]

When Reisenbüchler began at the Hungarian state film studio, Pannonia, he knew almost nothing about animation. Likely inspired by his love of Sergei

DOI: 10.1201/9781003214724-4

Eisenstein's theories about montage, Reisenbüchler found an ideal technical outlet via collage. And unlike most of his colleagues – who came to the studio daily – Reisenbüchler primarily worked at home on his kitchen table.

Reisenbüchler's collage works explode on the screen. His worlds are so dense and multi-layered that you feel they continue expanding beyond the frame. His vibrant and influential films, not so well known internationally, are often politically and socially engaged. They aggressively dive into ecological, religious, and assorted social (notably hyper-consumerism) and political issues. His work is, alongside Larry Jordan's, one of the early examples of an animator making full-on collages in almost every frame using a combination of historical and contemporary images.

A self-described "hippie with torn trousers," Reisenbüchler's films all contain a common thread of cynicism towards the world. Many of his works start with some utopian vision that quickly collapses. Reisenbüchler doesn't appear to deal with specific global or national events but instead looks at the larger picture, the endless cycle of violence, death, apathy, and greed throughout human history.

> All my films are linked to the same problem: they all express a fear of inner human qualities, of spiritual and cultural values. I feel that today, when there are so many alarming problems on a global scale, art has a duty, first and foremost, to keep alive the humanist approach to life that is the cornerstone of all civilisation. As for me, my films are born out of an inner compulsion to take a personal stand.[3]

Reisenbüchler's initial collage films are interesting, albeit unspectacular. *A Portrait from our Century* (1965), which uses a mix of montage and collage to trace a man's life from childhood to adulthood, lacks the intensity, complexity, and detail of his later collage films. There is already a hint of familiar themes. Through the man's life, Reisenbüchler attempts to capture the instability and anxiety of living in the 20th century.

After the masterful cut-out film, *The Kidnapping of the Sun and the Moon* (1968), Reisenbüchler made a rare (for that time) animated music video. Similar in style to *A Portrait from Our Century*, *When I Was a Kid* (1969) mixes drawings with many collage elements (landscapes, faces, heads, cut-out shapes taken from assorted illustrations and images). It's a striking, beautiful piece that explodes with colour, but collage serves more as a supporting player to the vivid drawings and cut-outs.

The Age of the Barbarians (1970) might be Reisenbüchler's masterpiece – okay, it's the one that socked me the hardest. Reisenbüchler's films are not remotely easy to decipher. They demand multiple screenings even to begin to scrape past the surface. This explosive kaleidoscopic wonder mixes various landscapes and architecture fused with cut-out images of cars, sculptures, war, casinos, and ads. "I cut the photos, which I have photographed from postcards into small slices and transform them into graphics," Reisenbüchler told a journalist in 1969. "This solution allows me to fit together pictorial ideas, or even several ideas within one image."⁴

The Age of the Barbarians serves up a vomiting rainbow collision of haves and have-nots. Behind all the material seduction, Reisenbüchler wants us to see the real human costs of so-called progress. And barbarians here have multiple meanings. Yes, there's the endless cycle of violent barbarians. Still, Reisenbüchler also seems to comment on the barbarian nature of advertising, the brutal ways of capitalism that freely destroys everything in its path for a little more profit. In the end, we see rows and rows of dead bodies. Nothing good can come until we stop racing *there* and start embracing *here*.

For those who are not me, *The Year of 1812* (1972) is frequently marked as one of Reisenbüchler's most notable achievements. Don't get me wrong, it's a good one. It is beautifully designed, paced, and scored (thanks, Tschaikovsky). Mixing references to the war between Napoleon and Russia with Tolstoy's novel, *War and Peace*, Reisenbüchler explores the devastating toll of war but goes deeper into the ideological differences (French enlightenment vs Orthodox Christianity) of the two warring nations.

Using collage materials (Orthodox and Christian iconography mixed with cut-out images of Napoleon and other historical figures) elevates the film from a specific historical context into a universal story about war, mortality, and anxiety. The aggressive use of collage and montage also creates a sense of never-ending movement. "Montage," writes Paul Morton, "is configured here as history, as a force that upsets the purity of this stillness and all that it can reveal."⁵

History is not still; it's continually moving forward, bowling over the present while feeding the future. We never learn, Reisenbüchler seems to suggest. We repeat the same damn mistakes – all in the name of *isms* and other idiocies.

Although Reisenbüchler left us in 2004, he left behind several interviews that give us insight into his creative approach. In this 1976 interview, he discusses his motivations using a scene from *The War of 1812 (you can find the film and some of Reisenbüchler's other works on YouTube)*:

> The plot has reached a dramatic turning point. The motifs of the Marseillaise in the music signal the enemy's approach. The Russian people are defenceless and frightened. We see a lone rocky pillar behind it, a desolate landscape with clouds, and a face with a shocked expression. So: the rock is a photograph of an Icelandic cliff, the Russian clouds of a distinctive brownish-reddish colour not seen anywhere else are painted by me from personal experience, the landscape is a picture of the Grand Canyon from a brochure, and I cut out a portrait of a Russian peasant staring into space from a Repin reproduction.⁶

The science-fiction collage film, *Moon-Flight* (1975), mixes original illustrations, collaged photos, and designs. Reisenbüchler was inspired by some space hypotheses he was reading in the late 1960s. One such theory suggested that the moon could be an abandoned spaceship covered in dust.

Ok then.

Armed with that spacey idea, Reisenbüchler created a contemporary fairy tale. "I wondered what a cosmic spaceship the size of the moon would look like, how it would be built, who would inhabit its interior, what role an artificial body of this size could play in space. I think this is an interesting game for all animators. By showing the construction of the moon, I wanted to put faith in the supposed creative forces at work in our galaxy."[7]

We see Tibetan figures and landscapes before a mystery portal opens, and we find ourselves in space, greeted by continual zooms through planets and landscapes, an imagined galaxy.

The detail of the collage work is extraordinary, filled with a beautiful mix of images: faces, planets, shapes, colours, and graphic designs. *Moon-Flight* utilizes a combination of zooms, stop motions, and occasional scenes that bring to mind Terry Gilliam's cut-out figures.

As mesmerizing as the imagery is, *Moon-Flight* is a tough nut to crack and seems to repeat the same cautionary tales of progress and the fruitless search for utopia. Whatever paradise we find, we'll inevitably ruin.

In an interview about *Moon-Flight*, Reisenbüchler provides one of the most detailed and insightful descriptions of his collage process. It's long, but it's worth sharing:

> I read a lot, take notes, and spend a lot of time in libraries. After a week or two, I put hundreds of ideas and sketches on paper, and in about three months I have the structure of the film I want to make. Then I start buying my collage materials. Six to eight weeks of searching in various bookstores and antiquarian bookshops. For my science fiction film, I also bought text-books on natural science, geodesy and astronautics to accompany the art albums, because I arrange my compositions from these colourful, cut-out images. I have to feel which one to choose based on my outline ideas. It takes 70–100 books and magazines to make a twelve-minute film. Over the course of about two months, I flick through and cut out the parts of this still dead pile that have stuck with me for some reason. I then group them together, organise them in binders, and then an exciting, totally subjective activity, a game takes place. I take, for example, a bear's head, a few snail shapes, a flower, and see what comes to my mind. I don't use a script, I write the story of my film in free verse. 1. Tibetan plateau 2. An eagle vulture flies across the mountains from left to right 3. Three yaks stand, behind them a barren rock ... And so on. And when I know that the first ten sentences are about Tibet, I start to sort out rocks, stones, crystals and animal

eyes from the raw material I have laid out, and arrange them for the time being against a white background. I am savouring the style of the film. I make three or four variations of key scenes, shoot them and then decide on the editing table which is the best solution. My eyes see something different in the - essentially - lifeless, colourless, brownish-white mass of paper than those of a possible assistant, so I do the graphic design of the film all by myself. On my desk I stack hundreds and hundreds of variations of cutouts, and yet I often end up throwing my entire day's work into the stove in the evening.[8]

Panic (1978) returns to the sci-fi realm of *Moon-Flight*, this time following a group of aliens who arrive on earth to do experiments on humans. The film (a mix of cut-outs with collage elements) begins with original cutout illustrations of an island setting near a body of water. Soon, an alien ship lands and starts beaming the island occupants up. The ship then flies through urban landscapes littered with corporate logos, advertising imagery, and a clutter of buildings. Chaos ensues when the Air Force and what appears to be a Godzilla-like creature attempt to fend off the aliens. Once again, Reisenbüchler sets his sights on technology, progress, and consumerism while mocking the idea that nature can be harnessed.

Through the 1980s and 1990s, Reisenbüchler would turn to films, primarily cut-out works based on his art. He would make three more collage films *Ecotopia* (1992), *Merry Apocalypse* (1999), and his final work, *The Advent of Light* (2002). All three films explore Reisenbüchler's favourite themes: consumerism, environmental destruction, and materialism.

In *The Advent of Light*, Reisenbüchler gives us a world with no value, ethics, or soul (think Idiocracy). The film opens with a montage of black and white imagery that shifts to coloured collage materials (including references to Stanley Kubrick's works) depicting a wide range of pop culture imagery. It's a world of chaos, lacking any sense of direction or, really, humanity. It's not a world of reality, society, or experience; Reisenbüchler gives us a world of grotesque representations of phony, hollow, funhouse mirrors. There is no centre to grab hold of. Everything is fast and fleeting, gone as fast as it appears – a disposable and facile world. There are references to artificial human breeding and conspiracy theories. In the end, hope appears in the form of sub-humans who rise against the soul suckers that have wreaked havoc on the 20th and 21st centuries. "It is a film about the bankruptcy of the over-mature and decadent capitalist system that surrounds us," said Reisenbüchler in a 2002 interview. "We are so degenerate. I imagine the future as a surrealistic fairy tale."[9]

Reisenbüchler envisioned *The Advent of Light* as his final work. "It is a synthesis of my life's work. The alienation from a materialistic outlook on life, and nowadays the fear of the harsh globalization of human values and the life matter of the whole planet. These are my reflections, and this film reflects them."[10]

Reisenbüchler's vision becomes somewhat darker and somewhat repetitive with each film. Yes, we get that the world can be awful, but what's the solution beyond repeatedly slamming capitalism and the usual targets? And let's not forget the irony that the very materialism that Reisenbüchler critiques is also the same one providing him with the mass materials he uses for his counter-culture films. That said, Reisenbüchler's cynicism about the world's direction has proved to be valid. We live in a world that feeds us the surface, not the essence. "How can we expect our offspring to be constantly renewed intellectually – as the future will force everyone to be – if they are given an inadequate intellectual diet from an early age? The minds of the whole of humanity are being manipulated by mindless kitsch."[11]

FRANK AND CAROLINE MOURIS (U.S.A.)

If Terry Gilliam is the most recognizable collage animator, then Frank Mouris' *Frank Film* is perhaps the most famous collage animation film. It was the first collage animation to win an Academy Award, and Mouris took collage into a slightly different realm: the autobiography. While most of the collage animators we've explored have used the technique to critique or mock society and power or reject logic, Mouris (in a different way than Jordan) uses collage to uncover or sort out his state of being.

> "Derek Lamb is to blame," says Mouris about his introduction to collage. "I had seen Caroline Leaf's *Sand, or Peter and the Wolf* (1969) and Eli Noyes' Clay (1964). They were both done under Derek in his animation class. I was just besotted. I had no idea how you did that kind of stuff. The only cartoons I ever saw were Saturday morning cartoons and all the Disney features. And I thought I've got to get into that class."[12]

Mouris eventually went for an interview with Derek Lamb, who immediately asked him if he liked to draw. Mouris, ever honest, said, "not particularly."

Mouris did not get into the class.

Meantime, Mouris had become fascinated by the collage work of Stan VanDerBeek. "Oh! I could do that! Anyone could do that!" Mouris remembers: "I started playing with cut-outs and was also really into the New Yorker magazine." Mouris was particularly fascinated by the absurdist, collage-inspired writings of American writer Donald Barthelme, who had been writing revisionist fairy tales. Barthelme was also creating his own collages. One in particular, *The Venus of Akron* (1970), caught Mouris' attention: "It was a headless armless woman perched on top of a car tire. I thought surrealism and collage; I could do that. So I just started collecting magazines. I love the idea of 'recycling' found imagery from magazines. I respond to magazine photographs viscerally; I am their ideal consumer."

Mouris found his material, well, everywhere. Aside from magazine subscriptions, he would sneak magazines out of dentist and doctor waiting rooms into an old schoolbag he carried about. "People gave me their old magazine," recalls Mouris. "I found some on the street on rubbish day. One day in Los Angeles, walking the dog, I found a paper bag full of porno mags. One showed that an actor we were using for my AFI thesis short film had another profession."

One of the first collages Mouris created involved ripping up colours and textures from fashion magazines to create five-foot collages. "They were terrible," admits Mouris, but they were a beginning.

Quick Dream (1967), Mouris's first collage film, was made while a student in the Graphic Design program at the Yale School of Art and Architecture. Very much a student effort, *Quick Dream*, as its title suggests, is a free-flowing, improvised piece that shows a young and inexperienced artist diving head first into collage animation, just messing around and seeing what comes out.

Recurring images reveal overlapping hands trying to cover an assortment of timepieces, perhaps trying to halt time. The hands eventually give away to coloured paper and Avery labels before returning to an urban setting where an old automobile (seen in the first frame of the film) reappears before being covered by a barrage of cut-out photos of different boys and men likely taken in the early 20th century. These images suddenly give way to an attack of cats, animals, and insects. More appropriated faces and eyes multiply on the screen before giving way to a parade of contemporary images ripped from magazines of the time. As Mouris recalled in a 2020 interview:

> We had a class of 12. Our professor suggested we try this animation course. A chemistry teacher had his Bolex and animation stand and he was making educational films for his students. It was very basic. We made stuff without any feeling Each of us got a single 16mm roll of film. About 3 minutes long. We had 8 hours with the Bolex. And that was it. When our films came back it was enlightening. We saw how fast or slow it was. We wanted to add music, but the teacher said no.[13]

Mouris admits that the film was just an experiment, and he had no plan or idea and randomly grabbed images that he felt "might be interesting."

You gotta start somewhere.

Mouris followed that up with *You're Not Pretty But Your Mine* (1968), which takes parts of *Quick Dream* and mixes it with some new collage materials along with assorted songs, led by "But You're Mine" by Sonny and Cher. This time the collage imagery seems more strongly linked by parodies of love, couples, and beauty in all their incarnations. Mouris is becoming more confident with his image choices, editing, and overall pacing. Mouris also learned a lesson about copyrights. "I quickly learned that a film with a soundtrack like that could never be shown publicly without having paid hefty usage fees to the record companies. Still, it was a great learning experience."[14]

These two student films were ultimately rehearsals for Mouris' masterwork, *Frank Film* (1973).

Frank Film is an autobiographical collage that fuses two overlapping soundtracks of Mouris speaking. In one, he talks about the inspiration for the film; in the second, we hear Mouris counting down before reading off a list of ancestors etc. Visually, the collages are taken from assorted magazines of the day and feature a barrage of cut-and-paste images (animals, food, school buses, cigarettes, eyes, and Televisions) that Mouris connects with his life.

The result is a sensory assault that blasts us with non-stop overlapping chatter over a sped-up visual parade that races by before we can even figure out what the hell we just saw. It's overwhelming. It's annoying. It's refreshing in its celebration of the monotony of the 20th-century mind. It's as if Mouris opened up his head, reached inside, grabbed everything he'd experienced up to that stage, and tossed it on the screen. There's no filtering, no emphasis on life's highlights, just a non-stop stream of fragmented memories and imagery.

Using appropriated materials from magazines adds another layer, extending the film beyond the personal and into the universal realm. It's a portrait of modern society and individuals being drenched with imagery and the nonstop push to consume, not to stop, not rest and contemplate, but just to keep buzzing along to the non-stop pulsations of capitalism's sirens.

Mouris made Frank Film had graduated from Yale, but its seeds were first planted at the school.

> Everyone in the class had to write a script. This was the swinging 'sixties when everyone just wanted to grab a movie camera and make up a film as they went along. My only hope was to take Stanley Kauffman's oft-repeated line that every auteur's film was subtly autobiographical, so I decided to script the world's first blatantly autobiographical film. That would become *Frank Film*.

From there, Mouris collected any imagery he thought could connect to his life. "My only test was if I liked the photo, it must say something about me." Mouris then glued cut-outs onto cels and tested them on an Oxberry animation stand at Harvard University (where Mouris was working in 1969 as a Teaching Assistant for Derek Lamb's animation classes).

During those test periods, Mouris discovered that rather than going through the tedious, time-consuming process of "putting down individual cels, taking frames, pulling up that cel, putting down the next cel," he could instead put down a cel, take the frames, then put down the next cel on top and take the frames. Mouris was surprised to learn that stacking the cels while shooting added a new layer to the animation.

> Because no cel is entirely transparent, the previous imagery would eventually 'fade out' as if the whole scene had been painstakingly filmed as a complex sequence of fade-ins and fade-outs. I never used table moves on the Oxberry. I did occasionally zoom in or out, if only to keep the imagery from looking so static. But basically, any moves were in the artwork.

Being a hoarder turned out to be useful for Mouris. "I often had the same magazine ad in different sizes, since back then there was a size variation in magazines, so that a tiny version could come from *Reader's Digest*, a normal version could come from *Time* magazine, and a giant version could from *Life* magazine. I only used original magazine photos."

From there, *Frank Film* went on to win the Grand Prize at the 1973 Annecy International Animation Film Festival. *Frank Film* was awarded the Academy Award for Best Short Subject, Animated Films a year later. In 1996, the film was chosen for the United States National Film Registry by the Library of Congress.

While the Mouris' continued to make short films, live-action features and assorted commissioned works (including *Good Intentions*, a 1995 collage-inspired music video for the forgettable band, Toad The Wet Sprocket), they didn't make another collage film for 25 years. That was the *Frank Film* sequel of sorts, *Frankly Caroline* (1998). This time, Caroline tries to tell her story but is constantly interrupted by Frank. While the film lacks the organic, off-the-cuff vibe of *Frank Film*, it is a visually delicious work with collage images flying by as the Mouris' jovially bicker and banter.

Mouris readily admits that he approaches filmmaking "ass-backwards." While most animators come up with a story, write a script, record it, and do the animation, Mouris' process was "unconsciously, or maybe semi-consciously, to accumulate huge piles of sorted, cut-out imagery, and then try putting it together into scenes." He likens this backward approach to Marshall McLuhan's theory of the rearview mirror: that we know more by looking back than we do about this moment now. "Only Caroline's organizing and editing ability save me from doodling around forever. If not for her, I'd still be collecting, sorting, and cutting out magazine photos to someday make something out of, like *Frank Film* or *Frankly Caroline*."

CANADIAN COLLAGE

Given the National Film Board of Canada's (NFB) often innovative approach to animation techniques, collage animation doesn't appear in Canadian animation until the 1970s. Here's a grab bag of collage animation films made in Canada in the 1970s and 1980s.

Jean-Thomas Bédard, a virtually forgotten contributor to animation, made a series of animated shorts in the 1970s, including two collage animation films, before moving on to live-action features.

La Ville (1970), an early music video, opens with a red circle and urban noise before shifting to layer upon layer of magazine images: faces, cars, shoes, fashion, newspapers, currency, architecture, and food. More than just an anti-consumerist rant, La Ville is an indictment of urban spaces littering the planet.

This is a Recorded Message (1973), in the spirit of Stan VanDerBeek and Jeff Keen, contains aggressive bursts of collage materials taken from hundreds of advertising images. An astronaut falls to earth, giving way to different pictures of baby faces that grow and change. The scene is followed by a collage of watches that symbolizes the obnoxiousness of advertising while slyly commenting on time passing by. From there, Bedard explores gender identities, sexuality, and relationships and our notions and ideas about identity are projected onto us by marketing and advertising. The lush and inviting world of ads soon gives away to images of politics and war as if (not unlike what we encounter in Reisenbuchler's films) to pull back the mass media imagery and see the brutal realities, the actual prices we pay for materialist leanings.

The Bronswik Affair (Robert Awad and André Leduc, 1978)

A snippet from *This is a Recorded Message* fittingly appears at the end of *The Bronswik Affair*. This mockumentary combines live action and collage (assorted magazine and book images and xeroxed imagery). The basic premise is that television has lured and lulled people to buy stuff they don't need compulsively. Even though the joke runs a bit thin, it's a funny, innovative, and clever film. The influence of VanDerBeek rears its head again, as do the absurd moments of Gilliam. The deadpan absurdist humour also anticipates the American comedians Tim and Eric, who frequently mined old technologies to create bizarre sketches. *The Bronswik Affair* is also one of the few examples of collage used for a parody documentary and somewhat linear narrative.

Opéra zéro (Jacques Giraldeau, 1984) is an oddball of collaged images and sounds that incorporates paper cut-outs, photos, illustrations, xerox, etchings, and drawings. Inspired by Shakespeare's line about life "being told by an idiot, full of sound and fury, meaning nothing," *Opéra zéro* is an engaging piece of baffling absurdity that adds up to a whole lot of, well, nothing in the end. The Dadaists would have enjoyed this marvel of madness and incomprehension – a perfectly unbalanced reflection of an undefinable life ruled by chaos, fragmentation, and meaninglessness.

Variations on Ah! Vous dirai-je, maman (Francine Desbiens, 1985)

The calmest of the Canadian collage works, Desbiens' film explores notions of home, time, family, and the changing priorities and preoccupations of passing generations. Set in a living room, *Variations* mixes live action with cut-outs, xeroxes (a trendy tool of the time, as we can see from this patch of films), photos, sheet music, and an assortment of found objects (toys, furniture, dolls). At once nostalgic and sombre, *Variation* is a memorial for the passing of time, people, and absence. We can change, tweak, and update things all we want, but it will continue for time to pass. What cannot be destroyed is a feeling of love, family, and connection that carries on through the passing of time, trends, and people.

Kidnapped (Thomas Corriveau, 1984–1988)

A man who claims he was kidnapped is under suspicion of kidnapping. This intriguing film delves into a man's fractured identity using a fascinating mix of photography, drawings, painting, live-action footage, and collage materials. "The film as a whole is conceived as a collage," says Thomas Corriveau. "In fact, I wanted the plot to be structured around the two conflicting personalities of the main character, Louis Vincent, who is the victim of a crime at the same time as he is the perpetrator of the crime (I wanted it as a kind of collage for the narrative structure)."

The collage materials are primarily heisted from woman's fashion magazines and used to represent Louis's imagined version of the female investigator. "I wanted this character, Claire, to appear as a real person for Louis but as an imaginary character for the viewer," adds Corriveau. "Fashion magazines are a kind of altered world, better looking, almost like a fairy-tale."

Corriveau found that using multiple techniques complicated (it was all made on paper and 16mm film) but also stimulating: "I also used painted surfaces that I prepared to be cut-out and collaged on the images. Also some gift wrapping with patterns, cut-out drawings etc. There is a big inventory of all sorts of things I like to use. And the film was assembled in a very organic way out of that profusion."

PETER TSCHERKASSKY (AUSTRIA)

I was wrong about Tscherkassky. He fits in terms of his use of stolen materials (in his case, 35-mm film negatives), but it wasn't clear to me how he was collaging these materials. On the surface, it struck me as a process that was not using animation. Well, in the end, I decided to write the man directly. His response: "I print and expose my images frame by frame with hand-held light sources, including laser pointers and tiny flashlights. And since I work frame by frame (with several exposures of every single frame, up to seven layers – that's collaging), I regard my technique as an animation technique."[15]

So, there we have it. I hadn't intended on diving into the concept of "expanded animation," but well … let's dip our toes in a bit and test the waters.

Tscherkassky's take on collage is intriguing and unique. In films like *Motion Picture* (1984), *Manufaktur* (1985), *Outer Space* (1999), *Instructions for a Light and Sound Machine* (2006), or *Train Again* (2021)), he takes fragments of pre-existing film footage, combines it with other film fragments. In some cases, he uses pieces from different sources (*Train Again* incorporates footage of trains from multiple cinematic sources along with a clip from *The Shining*). In other films – and this is somewhat unique within our collage expedition – Tscherkassky uses fragments from the same movies to create a collision that generates a new experience. So, *in Instructions for a Light and Sound Machine* (which won the Grand Prize at the 2006 Holland Animation Film Festival), footage from Sergio Leone's *The Good, the Bad and the Ugly* is torn up and altered to create an entirely new experience. The spaghetti Western transforms into an existential nightmare as a cowboy is hanged but then seems to reawaken in a cemetery in a state of limbo (between life and death). In both *Dream Work* (2001) and *Outer Space*, Tscherkassky uses footage from the horror film, *The Entity*, and turns into a surrealist ghost story of colliding of sounds and images. "I used found footage like a dictionary," says Tscherkassky. "Every single shot, and every single detail within these shots serve as words ... ...What I try to do is compose and create an entirely new story with these elements."[16]

While Tscherkassky has said that he doesn't feel he's consciously deconstructing his found material, tearing apart found film footage reveals its core: a choreography of light, dark, and dust. In *Motion Picture*, Tscherkassky removes all the narrative/figurative elements of the Lumiere's seminal, *Workers Leaving the Lumière Factory* (1895) to show us "the particles of darkness and light that constitute the original Lumière image."[17]

More so than the other collagists in this book, Tscherkassky's use of collage reminds us of the illusory nature of cinema by erasing the figurative elements to show the muck, the scratches, dirt, and hairs that, over time, become a part of the film. It's like a book or a vinyl record. Over time, dust, scratches, creases, and stains become a part of their texture, their reality.

Encountering Tscherkassky's films is a bit – and I mean this in a good way – like sitting in a car with a kid who keeps locking and unlocking the door. It's a provocative, playful, violent act with no closure (well, at least until the parent explodes at the kid!), existing in this state of limbo. Tscherkassky's work continually skirts between figurative and abstract, never fully embracing one or the other.

The experience of observing the figurative and abstract dance, public and person, is also reminiscent of being a passenger on a train (or plane, bus, or car). Lost in a maze of thoughts (or, conversely, sitting serenely, basking in nothingness), you glance blindly at the window, sometimes catching a layering of the passing landscape with fragments of the inside of the vehicle. The result is a collision, a collage of not just the visuals but also the inner mindscape of the viewer.

EMMA CALDER (U.K.)

Although Emma Calder didn't start making animation films until the 1980s, collage was always a big part of her life. "As a child growing up in the 1960's in trendy but rough Notting Hill, I was exposed to cutting edge Ads and Pop Art. Adverts in Magazines and Sunday Newspaper Supplements used montage and collage. Portobello Road Market was close by our flat, the market was a collage itself, full of Victorian junk, hippy shit, and relics from the

Boar War through to World War 2. I spent most weeks on the market and learnt my early design education there."[18]

The collage influence continued through Calder's youth. Her bedroom walls were covered with illustrations and photographs. She also learned about collage art via Puffin Books, *Yellow Submarine*, Terry Gilliam ("like nectar to my 10-year-old self") and even her skating teacher's girlfriend. "She was a secretary in a Graphic Design Studio/Agency invited me to look round and talk to the artists, illustrators, and designers working in her office. There I encountered many brilliant pieces of work including collage, which made me determined to become a graphic designer, once I had retired from ice skating."[19]

In the late 1970s, she was further exposed to collage while studying Art Foundation at Chelsea School of Art. This happened to coincide with the rise of punk and assorted D.I.Y. creations. "We were there working in college opposite the BBC TV studios the day the Sex Pistols did their famed interview. We were shouting at them as they arrived. Punk ripped stuff up and we couldn't not be part of that. Xeroxes, frottage (Something I used a lot in *Beware of Trains*) all came out of that punky time."[20]

Another influence was the work of artist Eduardo Paolozzi. Calder attended an exhibition of his work in London in 1977 and was floored by his collage works. A few years later, in 1983, Calder (with Susan Young) made *1984*, a collage work composed entirely of original drawings by Paolozzi.

> "Paolozzi had paid someone to trace images from magazines," recalls Calder. "He gave us 100's of these photocopies. Which we then re-photcopied, enlarged etc. We cut up and collaged some of these for the cut-out sequences. Others were used as inspiration for complete animation cell sequences. We would base out characters on a photocopy and then animate them as we pleased or morph one to another. Susan and I created the whole narrative without imput from Paolozzi. But nothing was included in the film that hadn't been a section or a part of a Paolozzi photocopies."[21]

Before *1984*, Calder made some unique films during her studies at the Royal College of Art that incorporated collage elements.

lkla Moor Baht Hat (1981) uses a combination of paper cut-outs with various collage materials (worms created with photocopied toothpaste, ducks made out of potato prints and drawings, a gravestone made with rubbing and watercolour that was then photocopied). Based on a traditional Yorkshire song, this comic cautionary tale follows a young man who pursues a woman sans hat and ends up catching a cold and dying. Oh, but that's not all. His corpse is eaten by worms, which are eaten by ducks, who the guy's friends then devour. It's the circle of life and all that.

Madame Potatoe (1983) might be the first animated film made, in part, with potatoes. Using a mix of drawings, potato chip bags, a two pinned plug (used for the head of the character, W.K. Wanker), newspaper fragments and, of course, potatoes, Calder addresses the stress of remaining true to yourself in a society that prioritizes the image of success. So many of us feel pressured to tweak our persona depending on whom we're around. We often have no control over how others see or define us. Unable to deal with the pressure around her or control outside perceptions, Madame Potatoe finally says screw it and returns to earth.

Random Person (2012) is an online stop-motion series inspired by rather harsh circumstances: a man lying unconscious on the ground outside a pub. "I was with a woman a friend of a friend, in her boyfriend's four-wheel drive, waiting for a lift home," writes Calder. "Finally, the boyfriend got into the car and started to drive off, and I said, 'mind that man, don't run him over.' I couldn't see him any longer, and I was worried. Then the friend of a friend's boyfriend said to me. 'What man?' His girlfriend replied with a yawn, 'just a random person.'"[22]

Calder was shocked at the callous reaction. "If he is random, what am I? Then I started thinking about how my own life and activities were becoming more and more random."[23]

From there, Calder created a character called Random Person made out of a collage of fabrics, doll arms, and her partner Julian's hair. The various films (about 40 episodes) that followed are likely closer to assemblage in that Calder collects an assortment of found objects (dice, teddy bears, puzzles and assorted miniature domestic items and materials made for dollhouses and other kid's toy environments). Still, Calder's use of found objects is at times reminiscent of how so many collage animators have used advertising imagery in their films. The fusion of sources manufactures a real and unreal world. In this schizoid landscape, all sense of self and purpose is confused and mingled with mass media and advertising's phony projections of impossible utopias.

Boudica A Norfolk Story (2013)

Commissioned by Norfolk Museums and Archaeology Service, *Boudica* follows the failed rebellion against the invading Romans led by the Queen (Boudica) of the ancient British Iceni Tribe. Calder again incorporates an array of collage elements, including flat models with paper collages made from photos of old Celtic and Roman coins, cut-out photos of an original mosque, and assorted photos of heads of statues taken at a museum. "They gave me bits of Iron Age pottery and old broaches," adds Calder. "They gave me photos of Roman coins and iceni coins. Which I cut out and coloured for the characters."[24] There are also drawn, stop motion and cut-out sequences. The Boudica character was created out of a piece of broken pottery that Calder found near the River Thames. Calder created the face with watercolours and then used twisted gold wire for the arms and legs.

Everyone Is Waiting for Something to Happen (2014)

Calder saw an ad for a competition called ReelLives. They were seeking mini-biographies of someone's social media image. The main requirement was that all the material (aside from the soundtrack) be taken from the subject's social media content. Calder settled on her animator friend, Richard Wright, as the subject. Wright had been flooding social media with what Calder describes as "annoying and anarchic humour." One day, though, he just vanished from social media. It turned out that he was battling bowel cancer.

Wright eventually returned to social media, using it as therapy. He began posting obsessively about cooking and baking.

Visually, as mandated by the competition, the entire film is a digital collage compromised solely of photos, images, and texts taken from Wright's social media accounts. It's a funny, heartfelt, and unique portrait of an ailing man using social media and humour to deal with a life-threatening illness.

Collage materials serve as a fun house mirror of the wild, free-flowing, and sort of uncontrollable concept of identity on social media. It's as though we're all less than minor celebrities, defined solely by our performances (i.e. posts, links, photos, comments). Who we become is out of our hands.

Beware of Trains (2022)

An unsettling take on the mental health of a woman suffering from anxiety, obsession, and some general personality disorders. During a therapy session, the woman recounts her main habits: a dying father, a chance meeting with a stranger on a train, her daughter's well-being, and a murder she dreams she committed. Her preoccupations are so intense that she's losing sight of what's real and imagined.

Calder beautifully mirrors the woman's fragmented inner state through a magnificent blend of collage, cut-outs, objects, and live-action. This free-wheeling mix of techniques creates an unbalanced viewing experience, injecting us into the woman's confused state of being.

Calder has crafted not just a bold and empathetic take on an individual's torment but also an apt reflection of a society struggling to keep it together in the face of overwhelming anxiety, uncertainty, and paranoia.

In terms of collage materials, what stands out for most viewers are the eyes of the character. You can't, you know, take your eyes off of them. "The collaged eyes give the character that stalkerish look that would not be the same if I'd have drawn them," says Calder. "I wanted to focus the viewer mainly on her eyes, and I couldn't think of a more effective way of doing that."[25]

Adding to the intrigue is much of the collaged materials are connected with Calder and her family. The eyes and lips are taken from Calder and her children. An envelope that the protagonist kisses belonged to Calder's mother. And much of the room's background material comes from old catalogues that Calder's mother-in-law owned.

For Calder, these diverse yet personal materials "adds a secret history to the work."[26] These photo materials not only add a layer of realism but also have a familial angle that reflects the main character's anxiety about her own family. You can see family – at least Calder's – in the face of the woman.

Even the scenes with trains were primarily collaged. "Because of Covid," says Calder, "we used my very small studio. We used a mixture of model trains, collaged trains, and real interior train shots."[27]

Ultimately, the collage elements keep the viewer – like the protagonist – unbalanced and unstable, always trying to figure out what's real and what needs to be improved.

Given her lifelong fascination with collage art in all shapes, sizes, and vehicles, what precisely about collage intrigues Calder so much?

> The combination of art and ephemera is an interesting mix and appropriate in these days of throw away culture, multi-tasking and channel hoping. When I start a collage, I don't know what will happen next, it lets me rest my brain. Having a method of chance creation is always a useful tool in the creative process. I'm not that great at drawing, so anything I can do to make something look good and original I do. It might be collage or it might be inventing a new technique. I use collage to help create concepts. By putting together random photos and drawing into the artwork, it helps me form stories and characters.[28]

LEWIS KLAHR[29] (U.S.A.)

I spent the happiest moments of my childhood at my grandparent's home. My metal cabinets of memories contain many folders of the sights, sounds, and smells of those days. They sometimes feel so real, so close, so clear. Yet, they aren't; I'm not sure they ever really *were*. They may be from snippets of home movies or slide shows; or overheard recollections from other family members. How much of what I desired was real to begin with?

Memory and nostalgia are deceptive bastard siblings of fiction. They entice you to crave something you can't quite reach and might never have had to begin with.

A similar ruptured intersection seeps through many of the multi-layered collage films of Lewis Klahr. Within an assortment of found imagery (magazine ads, home movies, contact sheets, porn, comic books) and sounds, Klahr's characters drift through disconnected times and spaces craving a connection and ultimately a sense of self that, like a dream, always seems to be just out of reach even when its right there in front of them.

Since his debut in the 1980s, Klahr has created a consistently mesmerizing body of work that has made him one of the more influential and prolific collage animators (he sees himself as a "re-animator"). His collaged worlds are tinged with contemplations (among other things) about identity (*Altair*), childhood (*The Pharoah's Belt*), sexuality (*Pony Glass, Downs Are Feminine*), memory (*False Aging, Daylight Moon, Engram Sepals*), Greek mythology (*Lethe, Helen of T, 66*), and capitalism (*Circumstantial Pleasures*). These concerns are often cloaked behind the inviting guise of mid-20th-century American pop culture, notably film noir, melodrama, crime films, popular music, and comic books.

Collage entered Klahr's life via his mother. "She had bought this painting by the side of the road in upstate New York," says Klahr. "It was like a cityscape but with abstraction and collage mixed in. I grew up with this in my childhood home and hated how it looked. But it was like seeping into me in some way."[30]

The second introduction to collage came about during a high school visit to the Museum of Modern Art, where Klahr saw an exhibition of work by Robert Rauschenberg. "He took newspapers and had a way of printing and blowing up the imagery. Looking at them in the early 1970s, they were my childhood, so there was this immediate understanding., I always had an attraction to the past and to things that had been in my life somehow. So that was exciting for me to see on some level."

In the late 1970s, while watching a history of American avant-garde screening, Klahr encountered a film by Larry Jordan. "There might have been some Stan VanDerBeek films in the screening too, but when I saw *Our Lady of the Sphere*, I thought that this was something I wanted to try and that I had a strong feeling about."

Another clue that Klahr was heading toward collage was his propensity for saving things. In the Nimbus films (circa 2009), Klahr uses a greeting card that his parents gave him when he was a teenager. "I got that as a holiday card and just kept it. Now, why I kept it? I thought it looked cool. I don't know, it only took me 30 years to use it, but I kept it all that time. I think it was tapping into this idea of attractions I had that I didn't know about. And these things would ultimately have use/value for me."

In one of his earliest collage works, *Deep Fishtank Birding* (1983), Klahr used elements from a world book encyclopaedia from 1956 (the year Klahr was born) that his parents owned. "It seemed I was onto something in terms of what I wanted to move forward with. Jordan was using these Victorian cut-outs. Not only is it hard to find those things, but he also had that era covered. I was attracted to things from my childhood to prolong it and go back in time."

Klahr originally began making found footage films but was frustrated with the lack of control he had. "I wanted to be more narrative. I wanted to be a Hollywood narrative filmmaker, but I did not have the ego for it, or the smarts or the tenacity to hang in there with that. I was too weird, you know."

Collage cut-outs enabled Klahr to control both the process and materials. "I could miniaturize the kind of events that were occurring in narrative movies that I cared about depicting. And so I could make my own versions of it. I had this great freedom."

Although there are elements of bittersweet nostalgia in his work, there is also an interest in poetics and expanding narrative language. In a sense, Klahr's films are like poems or songs (in fact, his tendency to compile his short films into a feature-length format was inspired by records. His films are almost like singles he initially releases before putting those with similar themes or atmospheres onto an entire album).

Despite the lure of Klahr's frequent use of candy-coloured pop culture imagery, Klahr's films are not so easily digestible. His elliptical narratives can be challenging to interpret, but the misty pathway between films and viewers doesn't bother Klahr. He believes his films are interactive experiences that encourage viewers to supply another part. "It's not a riddle, and there's no right answer, but you that's part of the navigation system that an audience member ends up being responsible for watching my work. There are things there that guide you and take you down certain directions, but where you go is up to you."

There isn't just a dialogue between artist and audience in Klahr's work; there's also a complex intersection of private and public, memory, and advertising. How often are our memories truly our unique experiences? How much have mass images (e.g. film, television, internet) wormed their way into our brainscapes before mingling over to our memories? I can recall times from my childhood when I'm not entirely sure if what I remember was something I directly experienced or was placed there via an outside source (home movie, television, photo album, gossip).

> "That's what I like about the pop aspect of what I do," says Klahr. "There's this attachment we make to it as media consumers where it becomes personalized and at the same time it's not personalized and it's experienced by lots of other people, but it's processed individually by us. It's both first person and third person and I like that."

In keeping with that collage trait of mixing high and low culture while tossing the question of authenticity and authorship into the discussion, Klahr relishes the collaborative nature of his work. "It's not just me. I'm collaborating with the culture. I'm collaborating with all these other artists who have made things in a certain kind of way. They don't know they're collaborating with me. Part of what I'm charting with my work is that experience that we have in first world urbanized western culture that's oversaturated with this media absorption, I don't think we know a whole lot about how that changes our consciousness and our understandings. It'll take a bigger brain than mine to figure all that out."

Klahr happily exists in the in-between spaces, and it's often in those spaces where we can find some deeper semblance of truth. History is full of examples of fiction taking us to deeper truths than documented facts. To take from my own experiences, Nick Tosches' biographies of Dean Martin and Jerry Lee Lewis read like novels. Tosches – almost like a collage artist – layers documents, poetic imaging, and third-hand sources together. Combined Tosches takes readers to a deeper understanding of the essence of the men and their time than any straightforward work of non-fiction could.

> "Fiction and myth gets at things that document can't," adds Klahr. "Then there's aspects of the document in inside all these things too. They don't completely separate either. They interpenetrate and that's what I've always been interested in. It's like, how much stuff can I get in one thing, In that way I'm kind of a maximalist, even though I'm so limited in my means."

RUN WRAKE[31] (U.K.)

Watching a Run Wrake animation is like tapping into the unconscious mind of some extremely stoned musical genius. Utilizing bold line drawings, Wrake connects a barrage of imagery from diverse media and loops it with a brilliant sense of rhythm.

Run Wrake's earliest – or at least most memorable – encounter with animation came in the 1970s. Wrake (who passed away in 2012) recalls seeing an episode of the UK TV show *The Old Grey Whistle Test*. "They used to play album tracks cut to grainy old black and white animation that looked like the Fleischer Brothers." Animation had entered Wrake's consciousness, but it would be a while before he seriously considered it as a career. Most of Wrake's days were spent fishing, digging up old bottles and collecting material – little did he know that his hoarding would eventually inspire his art. "Found material has always been a big part of my work. I can't pass a junk shop without stopping."

After secondary school, Wrake signed up for graphics at the Chelsea College of Art and Design. Although Dada graphics heavily influenced Wrake, he says that music was his primary artistic inspiration. "I was doing graphic design but buying and listening to a lot of music and animation was a way of combining the two." The idea of merging music and animation was inspired by a foundation class taught by an artist who had made a video for the band Art of Noise. "That was the real catalyst. It was very collage- y – cut very tightly to the beat – and it just really appealed to me, that combination of sound and image tightly synchronized, so that was the real turning point."

At Chelsea, Wrake made *Interest* (1987). Wrake's love of beats and morphing imagery is already present in this fast-moving groove feast. "I bought a pile of 10p off-cut pads from a printer and made it up as I went along; the bleed-through marker pens provided an alternative to a lightbox. The track was added after."

After graduating from Chelsea, Wrake went to the Royal College of Art (RCA). The experience at RCA was a pivotal one. "Chelsea had no facilities really, all the films I made there were shot and edited in camera, super 8 and 16 mm, and then telecined to tape and music added. So, most importantly, RCA introduced me to the picture-sync machine, enabling the planning of a picture and its relation to a broken-down soundtrack. I learned how to break down the sound and create a map of the soundtrack so you knew exactly which frame the beat would hit, and that was the real revelation for me — that you could create images to replicate the music perfectly."

Anyway (1990)

Wrake's graduation film follows the same path as *Interest*, but the images are more vibrant and alive. Crowded frames of surreal images jump through the frames. Wrakes uses a barrage of heisted photos, texts, illustrations, and objects tossed in with his distinct graphics. "*Anyway* started with the soundtrack, put together using the record and pause buttons on a Teac 4- track tape recorder and my record collection. The animation was created with the broken-down track as a guideline. Hand-drawn, cut and paste artwork shot and cut on 16 mm film."

Jukebox (1994)

Following his graduation from RCA, Wrake landed a gig doing title sequences for a series of film documentaries produced by Jonathan Ross (Wrake would create several commissioned pieces that incorporated collage elements) before completing one of his masterworks to date, *Jukebox* (1994).

Jukebox is a stream-of-consciousness masterpiece littered with wild beats (including bits of Curtis Mayfield's *Move on Up*) and an array of looped, drawn, and collage imagery that ranges from the surreal to pop culture (an assortment of xeroxed and cut-out illustrations and photos of watches, celebrities, buildings and Wrake's iconic, "meathead" image taken from a picture of a slab of meat). Watching *Jukebox* is a bit like spending the night in a dance club: it's a lively, fractured ride through a world of paranoia, fear, and joy.

Commissioned by Howie B and Polydor Records, *Music for Babies* follows the visually explosive *Jukebox* with a narrative loosely based on the experience of being a new father. Beginning with the birth of a child and flowing into a series of original and heisted images and illustrations (fish, objects, dolls, landscapes, etc.), the film's rhythm is more subdued here than in *Jukebox*. Bouts of calmness, restlessness, and repetition replace fear and paranoia.

Rabbit (2006)

In 2006, Wrake's animation took a drastic turn away from freewheeling, abstract imagery towards more structured and narrative-driven work.

You know those Dick and Jane books, right? They tell the adventures of two little kids and their dog Spot (*See Spot Run*). They live in a carefree and innocent world. The illustrations, like the text, are clear and straightforward. Typically (of my juvenile leftovers anyway), I inevitably began to think dirty, dark thoughts about these puritanical little darlings: "See Jane do Dick" and assorted clever stuff like that.

Across the blue, a chap named Geoffrey Higham was a book illustrator who created similar books in England. Wrake, perhaps fuelled by the same unsavoury imaginings I had about Dick and Jane, decided to take Higham's original illustrations and turn them into a bizarre little film called *Rabbit*.

From the appearance of the first word, "muff," we know we're in for something different. A Dick- and- Jane-type boy and girl kill a rabbit running in a field. They take the dead animal home, cut it up, and out pops a mysterious little idol. It seems that this creepy little freak can change flies into diamonds, so as they dream of becoming wealthy, the devilish little duo decide to exploit the situation and entice the idol to create more diamonds. However, when their greed goes too far, the boy and girl pay the price for their wicked ways.

The story alone is nothing special, but fuelled by Wrake's clever use of Higham's original illustrations – complete with accompanying text to describe every image in the film – *Rabbit* becomes a disturbing and sinister atmosphere that recalls David Lynch's *Blue Velvet*.

The film's roots go back a couple of years: while setting up a new studio, Wrake stumbled across some abandoned items at the bottom of a drawer. "In the early eighties, I found a few dusty old envelopes containing a selection of fifties educational stickers in a junk shop. They settled themselves at the bottom of a drawer for 20 years until I rediscovered them."

The idea for the film came from this collection of educational stickers created by Higham. "They have an innocence about them, partly because they are for children, but also because they come from a seemingly more innocent time, and I thought it would be interesting to present them as they have perhaps grown up, in an age where greed is often regarded as a virtue."

Wrake laid out hundreds of illustrations to find a potential storyline. He found inspiration in the "I is for the idol" sticker. "I thought it was odd to illustrate the letter 'i' for children; it stuck out from the rest. I knew I wanted to incorporate some drawn morphs into the film, which led to the idea of the idol having magical powers of transformation. As a child, I was a big fan of the Moomins (books by Tove Jansson) and loved the Hobgoblin's hat, which changed any object placed in it into something else; I think this may have been an influence also."

With the concept in place, Wrake scanned the original illustrations into Photoshop, layered them into movable body parts, and animated them in Adobe After Effects CS4.

Despite the sinister story, Wrake was less interested in mocking these quaint images from the past than in placing them within the realities of the modern world. "In an age where the slow exhaustion of resources by an ever-expanding population is becoming inevitable, the simple nature of the illustrations, their content, and the world they represent don't seem so foolish."

The effectiveness and uniqueness of *Rabbit* stem from the clash between Higham's righteous dreamworld and the truth of human nature; we know that such a virtuous world does not and cannot exist.

The Control Master (2008)

Encouraged by the response to *Rabbit*, Wrake took another stab at narrative and found images. Veer commissioned it to promote their CSA Images collection of vintage stock art (taken mainly from mid-20th century comic books, magazine illustrations and advertisements). Wrake made the quirky sci-fi parody *The Control Master.*

Extending the themes of *Rabbit*, Wrake takes these innocent-looking art images and turns them on their head. Using diverse sources, Wrake recontextualizes them in his imaginary city of Halftone. In this innocent and peaceful American town, the inhabitants are comfortably living the good life of the American dream. The citizens of Halftone don't realize that Dorothy Gayne, a mild-mannered blonde, secretly protect the citizens of Halftone from evildoers. When the evil Doctor Moire gets his mitts on a powerful new gun and shrinks Dorothy, what will the people of Halftone do? Who will save them from Doctor Moire?

The use of ready-made materials is beautiful and fun but lacks the spontaneity, surrealism, and absurdity of Wrake's earlier films. Like a piece of chewing gum, *Control Master* is momentarily sweet and sumptuous, but then the flavour wears out, the gum is tossed, and the moment forgotten.

OSBERT PARKER (U.K.)

UK animator Osbert Parker has crafted a unique career as a mixed-media animator whose work has included CG, pixelation, assemblage, and collage. His innovative digital collage works have been used in personal projects like the acclaimed *Film Noir and Yours Truly*, along with an assortment of collage-influenced commissioned pieces for clients like Nike, WWF, MTV, and Budweiser. He's one of the few collage animators who has managed to do works that reach well beyond your typical animation festival audience as they straddle a rather tricky border between the avant-garde and mainstream.

Parker encountered collage as a graphic design student in the late 1980s at Berkshire College of Art & Design and then Middlesex University (where he studied with the likes of Joanna Quinn). In school, he encountered not only Dadaist, surrealist and assorted avant-garde collage artists but also the films of Borowczyk, VanDerBeek, Gilliam, and Mouris. At school, he made his first collage film, *Movie Montage* (1987), along with his BAFTA-nominated assemblage-driven film, *Clothes* (1988). The success of those two shorts landed Parker an array of commercial work, including working six months in a graphic design and advertising company.

Around 1990, Parker started working on *Film Noir* (2006). This collage work pinches an assortment of objects (toy cars, miniature furniture), fragments, and images from crime-driven Hollywood films of the 1940s and 1950s. The film was shot entirely on a Bolex 16-mm camera and used stop motion mixed with hundreds of photo cuts out. It's a playful homage to noir and its assorted iconography.

Parker followed up *Film Noir* with the equally inventive and ambitious collage work, *Your Truly* (2008). Taking an assortment of pirated material from magazines and mid-20th century Hollywood crime and noir films, Parker creates an extraordinary, multi-layer work that combines photo cut-outs with real objects in miniature sets created from physical objects. Composited splashes and rain were made with actual water and by scratching on the film stock.

For Parker, collage offers a unique way of communicating various concepts:

> We all know that taking elements out of context and putting them in another space or next to unexpected items can instantly create alternate meanings in surprising ways. I tend to do this by juxtaposing animated photo cut-outs with physical objects that play with scale, environments and situations to communicate different narratives. Photocollages are particularly effective, especially when montaged together to create humour, horror, psychological and erotic themes because a photograph conveys authenticity and truth (but the camera can lie).[32]

Sir John Lubbock's Pet Wasp (co-directed by Laurie Hill, 2018) is a tale about an eccentric English man and his odd relationship with his pet wasp. Lubbock would, apparently, not only let the wasp eat off his hand but try to teach the insect to read, paint, and learn the piano. Pretty standard stuff. Parker and Hill combined the collage materials with stop-motion and digital animation. "Laurie and I found this to be a typically eccentric British story, which we took and exaggerated using stop motion, cut-out collage from Victorian engravings and digital techniques which seemed to give it an authenticity and accurate place in time."

Timeline (2021) was created for the Migration Museum in London. The purpose was to uncover and explore assorted personal stories behind historical events. "Working with objects collaged together in unexpected ways inspired an experimental approach that allowed me to investigate the idea of a timeline as a physical object that could change form over history and evolve into the future," says Parker.

Made during the pandemic lockdowns, Parker combined photos he took during walks around London. These were combined with various collage materials (archive photographs, barbed wire, broken glass, and string). "These were real objects, and they communicated a certain truth, authenticity and a reality that's possibly more powerful when brought to life through animation because they are moving in unreal ways."

Parker relishes the surprises that collage often brings to his work and creative problem-solving. "These surprises and happy accidents, inform my process and ultimately transform my films and in some ways, myself. The great American philosopher, writer, and cognitive scientist Daniel Dennet wrote, 'Mistakes are not just opportunities for learning; they are, in an important sense, the only opportunity for learning or making something truly new.'"

NOTES

1　http://www.filmkultura.hu/regi/2003/articles/profiles/Reisenbüchlers.hu.html.
2　Ibid.
3　Antal István: "A személyes állásfoglalás belső kényszeréből." Beszélgetés Reisenbüchler Sándorral. Filmkultúra 1979/4, pp. 82–88.
4　Rajzfilmgondokról őszintén. *Filmvilág*, 1969. nov. 15-29
5　https://english.washington.edu/research/publications/animated-esperanto-globalist-vision-films-sandor-reisenbüchler.
6　Dizseri Eszter: Hitet tenni az alkotó erők mellett … Beszélgetés Reisenbüchler Sándorral, *Filmkultúra*, 1976/3, pp. 54–59.
7　Ibid.
8　Ibid.
9　Elekes Györgyi: Világégés és animáció Beszélgetés Reisenbüchler Sándorral, *Filmvilág*, 2002/05.
10　Ibid.
11　Ibid.
12　Unless otherwise stated, all quotes from Mouris from a video interview with the author, May 13, 2022.
13　Treasures from the Yale Film Archive Presents: Frank Mouris in Conversation with Brian Meacham, May 2020. https://vimeo.com/417590508.
14　http://www.movingimagearchivenews.org/keeping-frank-and-caroline-mouris-animated/
15　January 2023 email to the author.
16　*The Trace of a Walk That Has Taken Place – A Conversation with Peter Tscherkassky* by Alejandro Bachmann, *Found Footage Magazine*, Issue 4, March 2018, p. 31.
17　HOW AND WHY - A Few Notes Concerning Production Techniques Employed in the Making of My Darkroom Films by Peter Tscherkassky, 2002.

18 Interview with the author, July 2022.
19 Ibid.
20 Ibid.
21 Ibid.
22 http://emmacaldersmoodydays.blogspot.com/2012/05/random-person-1.html.
23 Ibid.
24 Email with author, December 2022.
25 Email with author, July 2022.
26 ibid.
27 ibid.
28 Email to author, July 2022.
29 More in-depth exploration of Lewis Klahr's world will follow in, *Dreaming a Way (of) Life – The Worlds of Lewis Klahr*. Boca Raton, FL: CRC Press, 2023.
30 All of Klahr's quotes are from a January 2023 interview with the author.
31 This section comes from a longer chapter in my 2010 book, *Animators Unearthed.*
32 All of Parker's quotes are from email interviews with the author in 2022 and 2023.

Pending Elliptical Ghost Perverts
1990s/2000s

5

JANIE GEISER (U.S.A.)

Geiser's collage films are richly layered and filled with diverse, often clashing and crashing materials. Geiser's work has incorporated stop motion puppets, cut-outs, video footage, live-action, and computer elements along with an array of collage materials, including flat objects (photos, diagrams, fabrics, etc.) three-dimensional objects (plants, old toys, photo albums, cutlery, etc.), and assorted sound collages. The result is an often melancholy and mysterious work that explores themes of memory, language, identity, and history. Geiser's films are often like seances with Geiser as our medium, our interpreter of various fragmented, forgotten voices and their discarded, decaying objects. Absence and silence reverberate through her work like eerie screams from ghosts trapped in limbo, neither fully here, there, or anywhere.

Geiser started in theatre making, among other things, puppet and shadow performances. She eventually added film into the process. "The films disrupted the space of performance with their flicker and their scale, and with their reality," says Geiser.[1] Film footage would be projected over her painted set and puppet protagonists. "The films strangely made the puppets more real while at the same time highlighting their artifice," adds Geiser. "In a sense, the film projections were collage elements in these constructed spaces."

DOI: 10.1201/9781003214724-5

As with most of us, Geiser encountered collage before she knew it. "I encountered collage through advertising and the magazines in my house, like *Life* and *Look* and all those things. Those advertisements are collaged. They're pulling from here and there, and they're putting things together."

Geiser's closest early experience with collage came while taking an art class in college when they were given an assignment involving collaging materials together. Later, she took a Bosch painting and added telephone lines in the background. But Geiser's primary interest was painting, drawing, and later, sculpture and metalwork. "It was kind of a hodgepodge," admits Geiser. "I really didn't have a lot of confidence in myself because I came to art late, so I went for things that were a little bit more like technique, control, or craft. I started moving more into this performance and puppet theater, and that really became my obsession for quite a while. And that in a way led me to animation."

Even before Geiser started animation, her puppet performance pieces often included found material. "Maybe I would use a real fork to be a shadow or things that I would find like lace or different things that might cast great shadows. I liked the way that these materials would sort of unpredictably change what else I was using. It was just really exciting to me. And I think what I have realized is that I need to disrupt myself the whole time. I just wanted something that worked against the sameness of whatever I was making."

The Red Book (1994)

Geiser's animation debut mixes painted backgrounds and images. The idea began as a series of small painted images she made in a handmade book. As she worked away on *The Red Book*, she got a bit bored by the sameness of the painted materials and wanted to add a dash of chaos into the mix.

Enter that bastion of chaos: collage.

> I began to bring other materials in—bits of text, a real key, and toy silverware. These collage elements energized the compositions in the context of this painted world. Their materiality brought visual depth and suggested a range of meanings. I was excited by the merger and clash of the found and painted materials. The collage materials also added a dimension of daily life and time/fragility.

Imagine you've got amnesia. You need to remember everything, even language. How would you find yourself again? What would happen to us? We are so defined, shaped, erased, and limited by language; what would happen if we started from scratch? What if you forgot English and then learned Japanese? Would that also make you a different person? Is that what Geiser is exploring in her dreamy cut-out feminist film noir, *The Red Book* (1994)? I have no idea (ok, *some* idea), but it got me thinking about how big an impact language has on our identity and how we look, move, and react. I love the quiet stillness of *Red Book*. It's about a search, and yet – unlike classic film noirs – there's no sense of anxiety or dread, just a sort of calm, matter-of-fact reclamation quest/process. Would a new language change a chaotic reactionary person into a more subdued and meditative soul?

There's also the issue of *who* creates the language. If women are learning a language that was created and shaped and reshaped by men, does it not clash and suppress their "natural" state of being, thinking, and speaking? I can say the same thing. I've learnt a language that was passed down to me. I'm inheriting the filtered channels of teachers, parents, friends, and other influences – all of whom acquired filtered versions of identity. So, who the hell are we then? Collages!? No wonder we're always in search of ourselves. We have no idea who we are. We fret about mind-controlling devices, but aren't we already imprinted upon the moment we're born? Can we ever find a self that arguably never existed, to begin with? Maybe that explains desire and hyper-consumption. There's discomfort, a snap, or a crack within many of us that we desperately seek to fix, but we're not sure how to fix it because there's nothing wrong to begin with. How can you find that natural state, that single, true identity, when it wasn't even there from the get-go?

Don't feel sad, though, because it's incredible. You're free to be whoever you want to be.

Where was I?

From there, Geiser was hooked on collage but also leery of having each film resemble *The Red Book*. She incorporated more found and heisted materials with each new movie until collage took over most of the creative process. "Using found or repurposed objects, photographs, and ephemera has allowed me to work in a highly intuitive and associational way," says Geiser. "There is something quite singular about really allowing the materials to speak to me so directly and to respond to them in kind."

Not surprisingly, the origin of each project often starts with found materials. "I've been obsessed with unearthing possible and impossible narratives from these found photographs, images, objects, ephemera." Geiser likens the process to a forensic investigation. "I investigate the intersection of formal artifice and real issues and emotions. I am drawn to the way that found and constructed images/objects function in the context of a fabricated world, and the relationship of the body, especially the female body, to this world."

Geiser's work is demanding of an audience. Eschewing a linear narrative in favour of what she calls a "spiral structure," Geiser often constructs meaning through image, sound, and time. If you're struggling to find meaning or clarity while watching Geiser's films, it's somewhat intentional: "truth is elusive, and the questions are often between the layers."

Secret Story (1996)

While the origins of each film differ, Geiser's starting point is often inspired by found materials. *Secret Story*, kickstarted by a gift of assorted decaying toy figures from the 1930s – specifically, a toy figure that resembled Snow White – Geiser explores the period between the two World Wars via the figures of a woman and her younger double (maybe a mother and daughter). They wander about landscapes rife with floods and war before ending up in a forest. There is a sense of something lost, someone ailing who perhaps dies by the end. We're never quite sure. Accompanied by the sound of rain and a minimalist piano, *Secret Story* is a beautifully melancholy work that combines old toys, photos, illustrations, dolls, plants, and fabrics to simultaneously unearth and breathe new life into discarded objects and the hidden and imagined stories they might conceal.

There was – as there is in some of Geiser's other films – a deeply personal element.

> The sort of Snow White figure just really seemed like my mother. She kind of looked like my mother as a teenager, so I just started building this film around her, thinking of my memories of what I knew about my mother's childhood rather than what she was right now telling me about her childhood. So it's like your impressions about who your parents are from these iconic events. So, her father had died; he had had a series of strokes, so he was like always falling. And so I found another figure that could be her father. And then, and then I came upon a, a doctor figure, you know, so, and because the first figure I had found was made of wood, then I was attracted to similar wooden figures.

Lost Motion (1999)

In the spirit of the Hitchcock "MacGuffin" (e.g., when a seemingly central plot leads nowhere, like the stolen money storyline in Psycho that becomes forgotten once we meet ol' Norman Bates) and David Lynch, a man receives a letter and embarks on a journey to the "wrong" side of the tracks in search of a woman – or at least the woman he envisions – he never finds.

Geiser uses small metallic figures, toy trains, maps, stamps, miniature domestic furniture, dolls, and skyscrapers made from an erector set. Ultimately, it's the search, not the destination, that matters. We fall short of so many dreams but as long as we dream, there's – I guess – hope.

Quite often, the look of a found figure inspires Geiser's thematic or narrative direction. "The guy just looked like he was waiting for somebody," says Geiser. "And I made this woman on the other side of the tracks who was maybe involved with prostitution. The prostitute dolls were actually ashtray dolls. Sometimes the objects themselves determine where the story goes."

The Fourth Watch (2000)

Anticipating the collage films of Stacey Steers, Geiser places a batch of silent film characters inside a mid-century (doll)house. The result is a nocturnal tale about lost, forgotten souls momentarily appearing in various rooms. Their flickering, eerie presence suggests a time and people in limbo, a fading, fragile world crumbling away.

Ultima Thule (2002)

A small plane flies through a storm, maybe heading (as the title suggests) to the farthest point North. The deceptive blueish beauty of the rising waters and cloudy skies repeatedly appear as temptations and warnings.

Mixing video, silent and animated film with more conventional collage materials (toy plane, watch, wooden toy figures, photos, and assorted diagrams and drawings, sound collage dominated by the sounds of a scratching record, a vocalist and maybe an airport announcement), Geiser creates a sense of timelessness and foreboding. Assorted characters pass by, seemingly drowning victims of a flood. In fact, the plane takes on an ark role as it soars the deep blue menace. The final haunting images leave us with a woman (a silent film character who appears throughout) fading into the blue vastness.

Terrace 49 (2004)

Here Geiser continues to explore the collision of video, film (primarily old superhero cartoons), and collage materials. Like *Ultima*, there is a sense that something terrible is approaching. Images of a woman's body drift between rotating images of a truck sliding down a hill towards a cliff, a phone on a desk that is maybe about to ring, etc. But rather than become more apparent as it moves along, the film becomes more fractured (the truck goes forwards, backwards, then upside down) and clouded. It's like a visualization of memory you can't quite snatch.

Ghost Algebra (2009)

A woman (represented by an old miniature rubber figure) traverses a mysterious and fragmented landscape (made of old photos, objects, medical illustrations, cutlery, a bird puzzle piece, rephotographed video footage, etc.). We're not sure what the woman is seeking, but she is mentally and physically fragile. The collage materials (some broken and in decaying states) enhance the sense of something missing.

Ghost Algebra was the first film that Geiser edited digitally. She's spoken about the joy of disrupting her process; this decision was primarily motivated by economics and her film lab closing. Rather than starting fresh with a new lab, Geiser transferred the footage and edited it. This led to a change in her approach to sound as well. "I realized I could do the sound at the same time that I was editing the footage. Before that, I always gathered sound and worked with a sound designer. And, sometimes, that was great and frustrating because they wanted to make their impact too, and they might go off in a different direction. So I just started making the soundtrack. I was a little nervous about it. Am I saying I'm making the sound design? No, I call it a sound collage. I don't say I'm a sound designer." From here on, the sound collages would be as important as the visual materials.

Geiser is adamant that nostalgia is not her aim when working with old materials. She's more intrigued by unearthing hidden languages. "What attracts me to these images and objects is what they carry from what they have lived. I'm more interested in using the latent power of these images to evoke emotional narratives that somehow speak to our time."

Let's take the seated female protagonist made from rubber as an example. "Her position intrigued me, as did her ambiguous age and the seam – the evidence of the casting process – between her two sides," says Geiser. "She was permanently seated, but then, in *Ghost Algebra*, she was free to move, albeit in an unnatural position ... that unnatural way of moving is uncanny, and somehow draws more attention to her."

Next up came an old Czech book of WW1 maps and diagrams. At one point in Ghost Algebra, the woman "peers into a bunker, and sees the centuries of bodies dwelling below the surface. She peers into the never ending history of war and untimely death. Using this artificial figure, historical diagrams and images of bunkers challenges the line between history and fiction, real and unreal, and somehow, offers me limitless possibilities to evoke something that I can't put into words."

Floor of the World (2010)

Using snippets from the theme of the famous mid-20th century radio mystery series, *Suspense*, over images of shovels, digging, dirt, plants, calendars, a descending elevator ("ground floor" repeats a voice), doorways, distant police sirens, and presumably dead figures (the image of the boy at the end of the film is a picture of Geiser's father), Geiser creates another hypnotically haunting collision of people, places, and eras all seemingly trapped (like a skipping record that dominates Geiser's soundtracks) in a sort of limbo, not fully dead, yet never fully alive.

Flowers of the Sky (2016)

Dominated by two panoramic photos slowly revealing a mass of people seated at some reception or banquet. In the first, all the participants are looking towards the camera. In the second, they are now dressed in robes and looking away from the camera towards a stage. In between, we see negatives, a house, and recurring snippets of trees and flowers.

As always with Geiser's work, the key is the in-between spaces. Who are these people? Why are they gathered? We keep waiting (much like the experience – of leaving through old family photo albums or any photo) for something to happen, for someone to do something. In the end, something does happen: nature, as they say, takes its course.

Look and Learn (2017)

Using 1950s school yearbook photos and images from photo books alongside an assortment of instructional materials (maps, assembly diagrams, etc.), Geiser explores our method of learning: looking. In classrooms, we all sit in our seats, looking at the teacher or the textbooks. An underlying tension echoes through the constant "scream" of what sounds like a school bell or alarm. School appears as a place of calm simplification and order, but the world starts to intrude through photos of assorted protests. Contrary to the deceivingly orderly nature of school, the reality is brimming with chaos, confusion, and constant motion. Life moves past you before you get a chance to grab hold of anything. No anchors are gonna hold it back or keep you from it.

Valeria Street (2018)

"*Valeria Street* arose from a found yellow Kodak box of 7 slides from the late 1960s," writes Geiser. "The slides depict a group of men centred around a set of documents at a conference table in a generic office setting." What's striking here is that Geiser's father is the centre of that central photo. For an artist who has been fixated on creating narratives out of heisted images and various materials, how do you work with a character whose history you – to some degree – know? "These slides just kind of appeared one day off a shelf, and I thought they were something I had bought at a thrift store, and I started looking at them under the camera," says Geiser. I'm like, "that's my dad, you know? They were business slides, they were slides of men at work, so I tried to approach them both as found material."

Throughout the film, the central slide images collide with maps, assorted found imagery, and iPhone footage of a chemical plant (Geiser's father had a relatively high position at Exxon). Valeria street was a street her father had once lived on. In a sense, it's a tribute to a man who grew up poor and had minimal expectations from life. "It was just me ruminating about his path, the surprise in that path, and where he started."

Beyond the personal story, *Valeria Street* also touches upon corporate boardrooms and male power, specifically the decisions made within those dull walls that significantly affect landscapes (i.e. neighbourhoods, cities, countries).

22 Light-Years (2021)

With echoes of *The Fourth Watch*, Geiser returns to a house/home occupied by desperate figures who come and go. It could be a take on homes occupied by different families over time or a comment on disconnected and broken families. Geiser's sound collage of mixed voices (including a ghostly chorus), sounds, and instruments (a barely audible voice – probably in a church – speaking as an organ plays) all add a haunting and sombre vibe to the affair. The inclusion of home designer software adds a jarring new collision to the collage materials and provides an apt comment that while software can create a house plan, it can never make a home.

By this time, Geiser had already reluctantly shifted towards digital tools. Although she had been editing digitally since *Ghost Algebra*, *Ricky* (2011) was the first film she shot digitally. Geiser was – and is – a reluctant convert. "It was unsatisfying to me. It just felt too flat. So I had this old laptop I wanted to recycle and] take my stuff off. I said to my son, let's smash it up. So we did and the screen has about six layers of lenses and filter filters. So I started shooting with that, and that was the key to me. I realized, 'okay if I'm working with these crystal clear images, I have to figure out ways to make it dirty, to get different kinds of textures and vibrations from it that are not what the digital camera wants to do.'"

With *22 Light-Years*, Geiser took it further and added computer footage to the collage materials (photo negatives, diagrams, patterned paper, and archival footage). For an artist who welcomes disruption, the clash of computer footage with more traditional collage materials is jarring. "I was manipulating like home design software, so it looks almost like video gamey. I love how virtual imagery mixes and doesn't mix with the other." While the computer imagery feels stiff, it fits nicely into the timeless nature of Geiser's work and the themes of disconnect and absence.

As with the films of Larry Jordan and Lewis Klahr, we are merely skimming the surface of Janie Geiser's diverse and endlessly inspiring work. Geiser uses collage materials as a bridge between the past and present, the dead and the living, and those without a voice. Her films' elliptical narrative nature traces themes of memory, loss, anxiety, and history. While Geiser's work is often deemed conceptual (and yes, it is), there's also an intuitive, "gut instinct" approach at play, often kickstarted by an image, toy, photograph, or whatever material speaks out to her.

Geiser's films are often pretty sad affairs. "I do seem to have a dark side. I had a pretty nice family upbringing, but, you know, we grew up in the shadow of World War II, the Vietnam War, and the Civil Rights Movement. Growing up, a lot was going on in my world, just like there is for anybody now." It is strange that someone creating a playground for adults, in a sense, who can create any world she wants, would make such melancholy works. Geiser admits that maybe she seems (and I'm sure many can attest to this feeling) always to be prepared for disaster. "There's something about the power of that negative imagining," says Geiser. "If a loved one, let's say, hasn't returned home, we start imagining the worst, which maybe better prepares us for the best. I think we're just a very unformed species. We're really fucked up."

MARTHA COLBURN (U.S.A.)

"We've all been doing collage since kindergarten," says Martha Colburn, one of the most influential contemporary collage animators.[2] Manic visual flurries might be a way to summarize Colburn's lightning-paced collage films.

It's like sitting – in a good way – with an ADD chatterbox that drifts from topic to topic before you can even find a crack of engagement, but once you catch up, you uncover films that address gender, myth, sexuality, power, and politics.

Self-taught, Colburn (who originally hails from Baltimore, Maryland) began working on found footage initially. "I was cutting each frame up of that, so I started collaging literal 16mm size frames. I'd work on each frame, paint, recut, but i was also cutting the time and the action, not just the image. So it was all at once."

Colburn shifted into collage and animation primarily out of minor necessity: she needed titles for her found footage films. "I was cutting up individual letters within a 16mm frame and trying to tape them to create a title. I finally said, well, I should animate some titles." After watching assorted Monty Python VHS tapes, Colburn figured, "Oh, it can't be that hard," and began embracing collage elements. During that period, Colburn also studied painting at the Maryland Institute College of Art. "I was doing all these paintings, taking Presidents and mutating them with paint, or taking old record covers or advertisements and subverting them to the best of my ability using collage and paint."

The decision to animate collages came out of a somewhat unusual place. "What I found difficult was how do get the [collage paintings] shown. I showed them in Baltimore, and they either got stolen off the wall [which seems fitting for a technique that relies upon theft]or lost or damaged. I saw that turning these collage paintings into animated films was a good way to have your work seen."

Unlike many collage artists, Colburn was somewhat particular about the materials she heisted for her films. "When I was starting out in the 1990s, we had a flood of material from the fifties, sixties and seventies to use. I can't say that I specifically collected that much, maybe certain things for certain films. At the beginning, it really was just an impulse to make things move around quicker than hand drawn animation, which is so laborious that it scares most amateurs, as I am, away. So the spontaneity of collage is really what initially attracted me. I'm a high energy person. I'm not gonna sit down and draw for that long."

In terms of process, Colburn has a unique way of creating her films. In the early days, she began making her films on the floor before moving to a standing position. Eventually, she moved to a ladder for a vertical multi-planed glass animation stand she constructed. The stand has two layers of glass and a background of indeterminate length. She suspends her cut-out figures on a magnet on the back side of each moving part, and then there's also a magnet behind the glass. This means that the characters cannot cross paths and inevitably face their demise as a new character enters the screen.

"They are literally floating collages," adds Colburn. "That's why you see a shadow, something which is normally the nemesis of animators. I embraced the shadow because I wanted that sense of realism. You know, you're in a real three-dimensional world."

In later films, Colburn's material choices became more focused and politicized. "There was more of like a critical discourse about what the materials mean to the meaning of the film. So, i'd use, for example, a pipe cleaner to give the feeling that that character is desperate, or that character is hurt. The materials actually had to resonate with the meaning of the film."

Even though Colburn's early collage films (e.g. *Evil of Dracula, There's a Pervert in the Pool, Can't Keep Up*) have a freewheeling and playful vibe, concerns about the world around her were readily apparent in those early works. Themes of sexuality, addiction, health, environment, and advertising all crop up.

> I was really inspired by this early film, *The Sinking of the Lusitania* (Winsor McCay, 1915). At the beginning there were films that were made to convey historical events that no one could see, like if it's a ship sinking in the middle of the ocean. In a way I wanted to recreate things that were happening in the world, but through my lens, through collage and paint and music to let people kind of calm down and sink it deeper into a thought.

Colburn's 21st-century films veer more directly into political issues, specifically the U.S.A.'s often complicated history of violence, colonization, political interference, etc., "I felt like in the 1990s was a cultural crisis right around me in Baltimore. I was in the middle of everything being discussed today: systemic racism, violence, hate, sexism, you name it, it was there. And then, I moved to Europe in 2000. That was a real turning point because I discovered a lot of European art."

After 9/11, Colburn eventually moved back to the U.S.A. "I really felt like I needed to be in the US to make films about the war and about the politics and about all the things I was reading about. I got out of my bubble that I gleefully was in. Now, I don't know if you can be, but somehow in the nineties you could be, because there was no social media and there was television if you wanted it. I just got much more engaged in what was going on."

Colburn's desire to deal with pressing contemporary issues also led her away from the tendency towards surrealism in collage:

> I felt so pressured by the politics in my life that I had to be a realist, which got rid of my anxiety more than an escape or a rejection of all that would have. I want my subjects to be recognizable, a document of the time I live in, sometimes the moment. I was working on topics of the moment, but using the slowest of art forms, so this caused some acceleration of my process. In the studio, it was a play between urgency and patience.

Another adjustment that Colburn was forced to make was related to technology. After getting a gig creating visuals for an orchestra, she realized that 16-mm film just wouldn't cut it. "The screen was the size of a football field and they said you can't work on 16 mm because it will be too rough and grainy when enlarged. So basically the practicalities of wanting to do something bigger pushed me into having to animate digitally. And then when you're moving and living on the road a lot, as I did, it's very hard to continue 16 mm."

Colburn has said that her films move "faster than a heartbeat" and that seems to be something that links all the films from the beginning to the end:

> If I have 30 pieces of paper moving around on the glass and the background, you have to keep it all moving. It's very different than drawing animation, where you could have slowly drawn like the flip of a tail or something. With collage, because it's cut out, it demands to keep moving and to be activated because otherwise, you lose the illusion. The illusion breaks down very quickly. I could only get this much out of this material, so the speed of it made it more magical to me.

Evil of Dracula (1997)

Fangs, blood, bats, and assorted vampire iconography vandalize an assortment of advertising images of people. Don't be seduced by the apparent surface silliness; Colburn ridicules how marketers and advertisers try to take the consumer's souls by enticing them with all sorts of faux utopian horseshit. A funny, punk assault on the evil of advertising.

I Can't Keep Up (1997)

This combination of photos, videos, and hand-painted cut-outs is a strangely riveting rant (by poet 99 Hooker) on anxiety, paranoia, and a world overwhelming the narrator!

There's a Pervert in Our Pool (1998)

A randy narrator (Fred Collins) rants, moans, and groans over a parade of distorted and fragmented imagery (anima heads, women's bodies, dildos) featuring some famous pervs (e.g. cops, Fatty Arbuckle, Rev, Jim Baker, Woody Allen, a muscular Bill Clinton) all gathered together in a backyard pool for a leisurely swim.

Spiders in Love: An Arachnogasmic Musical (1999)

Keeping with the rapid-fire/graffiti vein of her early works, this spider musical/scream fest (featuring music by Jad Fair and Jason Willett) is dominated by, you guessed it, images of spiders with women's faces, dildos, skeletons, along with splatters of painted elements. An explosive anarchistic comic death scream celebration of love, lust, and such things. I think.

Cats Amore (2000)

Featuring a soundtrack that sounds like someone trying to improvise The Stooges and Albert Ayler, *Cats Amore* continues Colburn's interspecies collaging, this time with assorted cat heads on female bodies, kitties with lipstick and make-up (painted on stolen imagery), and a bunch of pervy dogs enticed by it all.

Groscher Lansangriff: Big Bug Attack (2001)

One of several music videos Colburn has made (this one for German electronic artist Felix Kubin), *Big Bug Attack* features a litany of collage insect imagery (yes, often mixed with human faces or bodies) along with painted photos (historical figures, celebrities, the musician who made the piece). Given the recurring images of eyes, phones, recording devices, peepholes, guns, and bugs, it's got something to do with spying and a culture that loves to look without being seen.

Skelehellavision (2002)

Skeletons, flames, sex, painted skulls over photos of bodies, a demon cop, some s&m (sadomasochism) scenes, snakes, and a sound mash-up of a repeating jazz refrain with ghoulish sounds and assorted instrumental noises. Sex and death. An ode to death? A vivid, discombobulating reminder to get it on while you can? (although it seems that sex is happening in Colburn's version of the hellish afterlife). In the end, we're all just bones trying to bone.

Colburn found much of the material in a thrift store near an erotic cinema in San Francisco that had closed. "The rest is animated, flat puppets floating on glass over black and then superimposed with footage of a volcanic flow at night. I did those scratched pieces in projection booths and trains at night, on a film tour in Europe on a mini light box I carried. There are hand scratched skeletons on each frame and flames and dots and lines."[3]

Secrets of Mexuality (2003)

The eroticism of wrestling is explored via scratched film frames, objects, kitschy floral imagery, and found photos of Mexican wrestlers that Colburn vandalizes with hand-painted breasts, demon horns, erections, etc. Mashed to a frantic jazz score, Colburn's familiar skeletal imagery reappears (a nod, in this case, to Mexico's "Day of the Dead" traditions) as she explores that fine line between sport and sexuality.

Myth Labs (2008)

By now, Colburn is veering into films focusing more specifically on complicated U.S. history and politics. Beginning with an image of Jesus and what might be the landing of the Mayflower, the immigrants (some call them pilgrims) arrive and meet the indigenous population. When one indigenous guy kills a pilgrim with an arrow, a bible flies out of the dead man's hands revealing packets of meth, and from there, the drug spreads, creating havoc.

Myth Labs is about drug addiction, but Colburn also likens addiction to religion and how religion has destroyed many lives. The imagery (composed of complex sewing of illustrations, drawings, and photos) dizzyingly races by like a rapid, unpredictable addict to the accompaniment of a violent, chaotic soundtrack.

In Colburn's earlier films, there's always an element of comedy, but Myth Labs ain't funny. It's a startling, disturbing, and angry scream about religion, addiction, and politics. Not surprisingly, it also came from a very personal place:

> I went home for Christmas and saw Meth addicts at the train station- in the smallest Pennsylvania town, my best friend from childhood made it through a Meth addiction. I met her 17-year-old Meth-affected son, a new-found friend who is going to the Florida swamps to find her High school friend who's on Meth, another friend is complaining about her furniture-moving Meth-addicted neighbour and so forth. All of this came after making the film. It struck me that it was a rural affliction, and having come from a very rural area, I could understand the lure of the drug. That said, I have never done Meth. I found interviews with lumberjacks, farmers, the Amish, truck drivers, ministers and mountain people who were on Meth, and I recognized something of myself because these people are 'the cloth I am cut-of'.[4]

Join the Freedom Force (2009)

Made in the Netherlands using an upright, three-dimensional glass technique, this choppy clash of collaged materials and hand-painted elements depicts – and celebrates – a history of protest across the planet. It's like a lo-fi punk recruitment video that unites all the protestors and causes. Backed by a song by Knalpot, Colburn creates a sort of anarchist raw-raw mosh pit of cops and protestors.

Triumph of the Wild (2009)

In this mini-epic, Colburn, accompanied by an aggressive piano, races through the history of America and its favourite pastime: war. Here, Colburn frantically escorts us – more like we're being pulled – through various American conflicts: the American revolution, Korean and Vietnam wars and conflicts in the Middle East. It's a dizzy, overwhelming film that leaves you unsettled, struggling to make sense of the frenetic scenes of violence and conflict that race by the screen.

What's particularly striking about *Triumph of the Wild* is the innovative use of puzzles alongside numerous original and looted imagery and materials. "I realized there were some themes of puzzles," says Colburn. "I couldn't buy a blood puzzle, so I made one. Initially, I used puzzles because it resonated with the story I heard from an Afghanistan war veteran on the news, talking about how when he'd be driving. Then he'd suddenly be back in Afghanistan. So I said, well, a puzzle would be a great way to do that transition because it is kind of like P T S D, like pieces of reality are there and other parts are gone."

Working with a friend, Colburn would create the puzzles and hand them over to a friend who enjoys putting them together. Once finished, the friend would bring the completed puzzle back to Colburn on a piece of cardboard. "I would then take them piece by piece and glue them onto acetate as I took a picture. It's really the easiest thing I've ever done. I mean, people look at it and they think that's the hardest thing."

Triumph of the Wild is an extraordinary work that succinctly traces the evolution of violence and conflict from animals hunting animals, to humans hunting animals to humans hunting humans. In a compressed work, Colburn manages to touch upon an assortment of societal and political issues while asking us just what is the point of all this. What is the endgame of this endless desire to conquer and kill? Fittingly, the film ends with the appearance of Colburn's familiar skeleton image which quickly dissolves into black. There is no answer. Only nothingness. Until it starts again and again.

EDWIN ROSTON (U.K.)

Attracted to the carefree and destructive nature of collage, U.K. animator Edwin Roston made collages by the time he was a teenager and likely earlier. "My mother was an artist and art teacher so I imagine I did some college when I was very young. I was certainly making collages quite a bit by the time I was a teenager, as well as drawing – and combining the two. I guess it was a way of making pictures that seemed more open and had less rules or obvious right or wrong than some other methods - and so felt very accessible."[5]

Roston particularly enjoyed the combination of surprise and playfulness that came from tinkering with collage materials. "You could make images you could never get another way. I guess the chance aspect appealed a lot too, and probably making collage taught me a lot about how the element of chance could be an exciting part of making art."

The interest in collage animation grew from Roston's pre-existing collage art. He quickly learned that there is a vast difference between making a collage and making collage animation. "My collages had many layers and were built up and stripped back a lot along the way. I started taking photographs at various stages of making one. I felt that only ending up with the final image seemed arbitrary and unrepresentative of the process."

One of Roston's instructors suggested that he try to make the collage as a film. Roston agreed and quickly found that it required a different approach. As I started to make things happen for the camera, which I wouldn't have done if I wasn't recording it, but the impulse to show the creative process in action has remained a key part of my animation work to some degree ever since.

Roston's earliest films *Experimental Research* (1997), *Assault Reflex* (1998) *Tunnel Visions* (1999), and *Spectres* (2005) combine collage materials with drawn elements (using white correction fluid along with black markers and ink.) or, as in *Tunnel Visions*, with live-action parts. "I kept the process basic for practical reasons but also a limited palette/process helps when the work is improvisational and you're working unconsciously, which was my main priority," says Roston.

While Roston has a loose idea about a film, much of the process is improvised. "I accrue a big pile of images over a period of time from different sources, not a random collection but without knowing exactly how the images connect. I would then take the pile of images into the rostrum room to see what happens. Thats been the overriding idea with most of my films – to see what happens with a certain combination of materials/images/processes. Maybe to find out what the film is about (and what I am thinking) by making the film itself."

While Roston has drifted into other animation/film techniques, he believes that the process of collage animation has even more to offer artists now than it used to. "As a physical process, it engages a very particular way of thinking with the body/hands that I guess less people are engaged with as digital animation processes have become the norm."

Roston admits that collage has a different look in this digital age, where print media is slowly vanishing. Today's youth do not read magazines and newspapers like past generations did. "I have heard students say the idea of collage animation having a radical or political power seems very old fashioned, which is hard to disagree with," says Roston. "But collage animation has other aspects to it - there is a sense of intimacy and materiality that has certainly still has a power, and I think people still connect with it on that level."

Even if collage has lost some of that punk/counter-culture influence, Roston still believes it offers exciting things. "The issue of materiality in art has a new relevance today. It means something different to work with physical stuff now there is an immaterial digital world trying to claim all our time/ eat our souls, and also as the physical world suffocates in a deluge of detritus and trash."

LISA BARCY (U.S.A.)

Barcy has yet to make too many films, but the American collage artist undoubtedly warrants mention for her diverse collage-inspired works.

So, Barcy stumbled into collage by accident. "I didn't think that what I was doing was collage, but while working out ideas I would find myself appropriating material to fill in the blanks. Often this was limited to my sketchbook and often as Monty Pythonesque one-liners."[6]

In Barcy's earliest works like *Woman without a Past* (2003), *The Guilt Trip or The Vaticans Take a Holiday* (2004), collage elements are already in play as a supporting technique.

In her grad school film, *Woman without a Past*, which seems to be an autobiographical take on that complex notion of identity, Barcy mixes original drawings with vandalized pages of a book (apparently a dime store romance novel) and cut-up book and newspaper texts (the female character is primarily composed of newspaper cut-out outs).

"I go through thrift stores looking for potential junk all the time. It's my art supply store," says Barcy. "I found a book called *Woman without a Past*, which looked just like a romance novel. I painted all the pages black, and then I thought, why not make it a flip book? Once it was a flip book, I kept adding things to it."

Barcy started cutting text out of the book along with clippings from assorted romance novels. "They were phrasing things where they'd talk about the main character and they'd never give her a name in the beginning, but then they'd always refer to her as the woman. And which amused me, so I started cutting out all the instances where it mentioned that and just kind of, improvising little phrases and things like that."

The Guilt Trip, a stop-motion puppet work which follows Jesus and Mary on a wild and crazy road trip, grew out of Barcy's years in Catholic school. Barcy incorporates a wealth of heisted materials: cut-out illustrations of religious figures (Pope John Paul II, Jesus, assorted angels) along with newspaper clippings, paper dolls from old Dover books and various found objects (including a praying hands pencil sharpener).

During that period, Barcy took a stop motion class at the Art Institute of Chicago with Chris Sullivan. Barcy had been thinking about travel and road trip movies. And then during a visit to a hobby store, she stumbled upon an assortment of Tom Tierney paper dolls. "They had the kind of paper dolls you expected to see, 1920s costumes, Judy Garland etc... but then I see the Pope, which had be in hysterics. My mother's side is Polish so when we got a Polish Pope, they went absolutely crazy. Every Polish person's house in Chicago is filled with Pope kitsch. I could not wait to subvert and play with the Pope paper doll. And then thinking about the road trip film, the two ideas eventually merged into one."

Barcy attributes her turn towards collage and stop-motion to her frustration over her self-described traditional drawing skills. "While I'm glad to have that skill, it's a slippery slope to creating overly fussy, rather uninspired drawings," says Barcy. "I once heard Chris Ware describe this as 'constipated drawings.'"

Like Janie Geiser, Barcy is attracted to the disruptive nature of working with mixed materials. "There's something about introducing a completely foreign element to the mix that jerks me out of that headspace and opens me up to alternate possibilities. You can't go into it with a preconceived notion of what the final product should look like."

The unexpected and surprising nature of stolen materials also keeps Barcy from being too organized or rigid with her narratives. "If I think 'what I need here is a giant refrigerator' and head over to the refrigerator file then I've closed myself off to other narrative possibilities. Finding unexpected materials often becomes the prompt for a film. It's like playing with my toys. Kid's just make up stories as they go along, which is usually how I start."

Grub (2010)

A flipbook-inspired animation that combines the rapid turning of random pages from a 1930s farmer's book about pesticides overlaid with drawings that depict some gross insect that forms, turns into a muffin, and gets eaten. That transitions into an insect that ends up part of a not-so-enticing sandwich. "I had recently listened to this interview with someone who had been advocating eating insects as an alternate source of protein," recalls Barcy. "So I was thinking about this phenomenon, thinking, you know, it's not going to happen, but what would that be like? And just, again, it came from this place of improvising."

Turbulence (2010)

An intriguing cross between Terry Gilliam, Larry Jordan and a Twilight Zone episode, *Turbulence* is a collage short (Barcy made it with Depaul College students) framed in an airplane window. As the window opens, we see a mish-mash of tourist landscapes (statue of liberty, golden gate bridge) before a gaggle of victorian-era tourists come and go on the wing of the airplane. A man appears with a sign warning that "the end of is near" just before a fire-breathing creature appears. From there, we're greeted by an assortment of rather odd collaged images (illustrations and vintage folders of people, animals, landscapes, ships, a fish riding a bicycle, and plants) that quickly come and go on the airplane's wing. The result is a light-hearted stream-of-consciousness piece about travel and tourism.

Forêt (2019)

A beautiful, upbeat abstract work consisting of mini-collages of various cut-out shapes and colours. The film – made from an assortment of different decorative papers – emerged from a series of small collages (64 of them, to be exact) that Barcy had been working on for a collage festival. Before giving out the collages to people, she decided to animate them. "I decided to animate them eight different ways, and I just put them under the camera and improvised."

The Ephemeral Orphange (2020)

Barcy's most accomplished collage work uses found objects, drawings, and diagrams along with vintage cut-out illustrations of paper dolls taken from a 1920s newspaper to tell a story about a group of orphaned children and their daily life in an oppressive orphanage run by a husband and wife. Each young girl dreams of a life beyond the cloistered walls of the orphanage. One day the orphan girls appear to have had enough and devise a plan to dispose of their surrogate overloads.

Barcy's inspired collage choices give the film a mysterious, magical atmosphere. Although strongly influenced by silent films and set in the early 20th century, *Ephemeral Orphanage* touches upon those eternally tricky borders between freewheeling youngsters filled with dreams, imaginings and hope and the somewhat deadened and stifling spirits of the adults:

> My grandmother had these paper dolls in a shoebox. They were so hold that the shoebox was made of wood. She had written names on the back of them and she had told me that the dolls came in a color supplement of the Sunday newspaper and that they were what poor kids played with. Sometimes you could buy a pattern for them or just make a dress for them.

Since male dolls were never included in the series, Barcy's grandmother cut out a male figure from a box of men's underwear. Barcy used that figure for her the man who co-runs the orphanage. And aside from the toy blocks, flat materials were used throughout for assorted furniture (e.g. the orphanage sofa was a cut-out photo image).

Ephemeral Orphanage is a strange, eerie and hypnotic piece that echos the subversive elements of Run Wrake's *Rabbit* with the wondrously offbeat menace and beauty of Charle Laughton's live-action classic, *The Night of the Hunter.*

JODIE MACK[7] (U.S.A.)

Film strips, weeds, concert posters, maps, boarding passes, jewellery, photo negatives, envelopes, dollar store gift bags, beads, books, blankets, puppets, floral patterns, fabrics of all shades and colours, computer memory boards, junk mail, and even a horse's kidney stone. All stuff you might stumble upon in a bizarro garbage heap, not animation films. The ultimate recycler, experimental animator Jodie Mack, animation's Dr. Frankenstein, finds beauty and repurpose in life's leftovers as she breathes new life into the forgotten, discarded, and unconventional. Mack's collages clash and collide towards a sense of harmony and unity.

With rapid-fire creativity fuelled by unfettered delight and rampant curiosity, Jodie Mack has created an eclectic body of work that bridges contemporary art and animation with an utterly unpretentious – to borrow from music – lo-fi, D.I.Y. approach.

After some interest in theatre (which occasionally incorporated silhouette and cut-out animation), Mack took Film and Media Studies at the University of Florida. One of Mack's teachers screened the likes of Len Lye, Norman McLaren, and Harry Smith and encouraged experimentation. "We had access to some old 16mm films that we would soak in bathtubs full of bleach and experiment with," says Mack. "My first point of entry into the idea of animation really was a painterly one. I thought of the film strip as a canvas. I'd work on the film strips sideways and then all of the sudden you put it another way and you see all the individual frames. You're just fumbling around chasing your tail until it makes sense. And there were definitely a lot of discovery moments that way."

After graduating with a B.A. in Film and Media Studies, Mack headed to the Art Institute in Chicago for Graduate Studies. There, she encountered animators Chris Sullivan and Jim Trainor. Oddly enough, Mack didn't take any animation classes in Chicago. "I was a teaching assistant for a couple of classes and independently studied my way through. I did work with Chris and Jim. Chris worked it out so I could shoot on the animation stand there, and Jim gave me a Bolex camera and a little copy stand that I still use. There was a lot of kindness there."

In Chicago, Mack created one of her first films, *A Joy* (2004), a commissioned piece for the band, For Tet. "I made it with this stained glass contact paper on the window of this apartment I was living in, and the landlord wanted to take it off. So I was chiselling it off and was like, 'Oh, this is so cool' and 'let's save this old, gooey crap for years, deteriorating in a bag and, you know, glue it to film.' That was all exciting, but then it became 'Woah, what do you do with this?' and it's all of a sudden a photographic medium as opposed to a painterly something."

Even though she was making camera-less films, Mack's interest in found materials went back to high school. "For one project, I needed to make all these palm trees on a big backdrop piece of paper, and I happened to find all these old telephone books. I started ripping out the pages to use as material to make the trees. Collage was a place I went to as soon as I started using the camera. I was excited by people like Lewis Klahr, Martha Colburn, and Stan VanDerBeek and seeing a lot of crude animation."

Mack also found camera-less filmmaking a bit restrictive. "I felt bound early on by the limits of what we knew as an abstraction. I was experiencing a roadblock with camera-less filmmaking. It was cool, fun, and exciting, but what is possible here? One of the things central to my actual experiments with camera-less filmmaking were the materials themselves, using colourful pieces of plastic and often trying to scavenge those materials."

Much of Mack's film materials are from her hoarding tendencies. "I think it started with, like, trash, and then I moved to domestic decorative objects, which evolved to, like, decorative objects in general." When she moved from Chicago to start teaching at Dartmouth, she realized she had a lot of fabric. "I took inventory of all my stuff under the camera to see if I could make a film. Once I saw something there, I tried out different things."

All of Mack's films start with *stuff*. *New Fancy Foils* (2013) emerged from a package she received from animator George Griffin. "One day this beautiful book of foil samples showed up and he was like, 'I think these will come in handy one day.'" A couple of years later, Mack returned to the book and turned out a film. After exhausting the fabric road, Mack turned to other unusual materials like dollar store gift bags. "The gift bags were in a phase where I was moving to 3D. I started shooting all of this 3D stuff and made a film for special 3D glasses and did some live action. That was a moment where I was really interested in light, how it plays out in these different things." Of late, Mack's interest has turned to plants and computer chips. "I'm on a utilitarian kick. Things, like computer chips, that are useful, but not necessarily beautiful or decorative."

This willingness and desire to tinker with almost anything tangible make Mack's work unique and refreshing. She eschews the standard paper-based cut-and-paste form (e.g. using old photos, magazine clippings, etc.) in favour of an assortment of unconventional materials and even a somewhat different approach to the notion of collage. "At some point, I moved from a collage that's within a frame to a collage that's like a relationship, a temporal relationship with the film itself. I went further out, back to Robert Breer and Scott Stark, who does a lot with flicker. He made this film with medical images of vaginas, trees, and stuff. Again, using flicker and, of course, with afterimage, all these things take on these impressions. I'm fascinated by this idea of a composite image that is only perceived. It's not there; it's a time collage."

Though technological advances have made collage (like all animation) less time-consuming, Mack says she's shunned digital technology to a small degree. "I've partially ignored it in some ways as far as the direct capture and projection of my films is, for the most part, on 16mm. I feel like the Bolex is my instrument, and I love working with it. I love not being able to see what I'm doing for 4,000 frames at least." That has yet to stop Mack from embracing some aspects of digital technology. "I started in the 2000s. Video has always been a part of the equation; with every film, there's a video, many sound files, video edit, effects."

Mack's work has also addressed our iffy relationship with technology. *Glitch Envy* (2010) is a playful parody of the changing notion of "junk mail" in a social media era. "It was a time when new media was taking over and that's where the funding was, in new media, and in many ways I saw the new techniques of new media: dealing with the data of a video or something like that as completely parallel to camera-less filmmaking. You know, like, camera-less video-making in some way. As my films moved on, I became interested in technology replicating what already exists. Like your razor-blade icon looking like the razor-blade that actually cuts film."

Sing-songs and pretty fabrics aside, there are socioeconomic and political undertones throughout much of Mack's work. The rapid flash-clash of patterns and materials hints at the volatile nature of capitalism and consumer waste. We produce, purchase, and toss without much thought about the consequences or real need, but also beyond that, Mack also finds some beauty in many leftovers. Her use of these found objects often leads to musings about cultural appropriation, technology, human labour, domestic economics, and the implications of consumer culture in general.

Jodie Mack's films are brimming with jubilance yet tinged with a hint of sadness. While Mack's films resuscitate the discarded and abandoned items of a wasteful hyper-capitalist society, it is a short-lived joy. The materials will still end up tossed and forgotten on some garbage heap. "Some of my films are little eulogies for materials. I think one reason that I'm interested in animation is, for one reason or another, I'm obsessed with the idea of death and want to make that impossible. And so this idea of resuscitating what's about to go in the trash can to reveal its energy and give it a celebration."

MIWA MATREYEK (U.S.A.)

One of the many shortcomings of this book is that I've focused almost exclusively on collage animation films. Using collage animation tools within installations needs to be further explored. Last year, for example, I encountered the installation work of the Korean artist, Yaloo, which incorporates 2D and 3D collage elements into her environmentally themed installations. Another installation artist worthy of some brief exploration here is Miwa Matreyek.

Matreyek is a Vancouver-based artist who started as a collage artist before shifting to animation (she studied at CalArts) and then to unique live performances where she performs with the animation material as a shadow puppet. It's an intriguing dreamscape that mixes animation, theatre, and digital tools with handmade elements.

As an undergraduate student, Matreyek soaked up as much art as possible. She explored photography, painting, printmaking, and sculpture. Then she realized she didn't need to choose a single road to travel down. "Collage became a way that I can combine elements of the various mediums (along with found images), as well as a way to play without ruining the original (by making Xerox copies) and cutting up and rearranging the images into new compositions."[8]

Matrayek was also inspired by zine-making and riot grrl/punk subcultures. "I was working with degraded images (made high contrast and losing details through a process of multiple Xerox copying) was interesting to me, and I liked how the black and white and grainy prints unified the look of materials that came from disparate sources."

And much like the early collage artists using the technique as a way of challenging painting, Matreyek was seeking a technique that would minimize the hand of the artist. "I spent much of high school trying to draw in an anime style, and often felt frustrated in college that the influence leaked out in the style my hands were inclined to draw. Collage became a way to get away from that."

After diving into collage art and creating several pieces, Matreyek felt something was missing. "Once I started scanning collage materials and cutting them up in Photoshop or Flash, I realized the next step was to make them move. My early collage animations featured objects that came apart and rearranged themselves into new forms, moving in rhythm to the music I was recording on a 4 track. I was also often inserting myself as rotoscoped figure into the surreal worlds of the collage."

Her earliest films, *Machine* (2003), *Digitopia* (2005), and *Grater City* (2006), combine collage and compositing. *Machine*, a music video, takes on themes of war, destruction, and decay using collaged backgrounds of various buildings in various states of disarray. *Digitopia* (made at CalArts) is a sci-fi-tinged work about the fusion of human and technology that merges heisted photo materials of building, recording devices, and mountains with compositing and drawings. It's a great example of the turn towards digital collage. *Grater City* is a funny work about a giant human cat that briefly menaces a city. Matreyek's interest in combining performance with other media is readily apparent. *Grater City* mixes live action, drawn animation, and compositing along with a collage of cheese graters that appear as buildings.

Lumerance (2012), a short piece about connection and desire, is another fusion of various sources, including collaged elements (an egg rocket, hand and lips mixed with various materials from the NASA database). If not quite matching my conservative notions of collage animation, it certainly is full-on collage-y in spirit.

Matreyek admits to being fascinated by the surprises that often evolve from placing diverse images together. "The simple juxtaposition of images can make your brain do a little backflip to make sense of unexpected relationships between unlikely objects, scale, shapes, colors, textures, perspectives, etc," says Matreyek. "I love the playful transformations that happen, and the giddy leap of faith I as the collage maker and simultaneous viewer must take – even more because often you don't know how the composition and feeling of the images will transform until they combine with other images ... there is an ongoing process of discovery."

As with many collage artists, Matrayek often dives into a pile of magazines and clippings with no plans to see where it might take her. "There is a sense of discovering treasures, intuition, and getting into a flow, getting excited about the combinations of images and the new meaning that can emerge. I love working with collage in various compositional ways. Sometimes I love making visually busy collages that give no point of rest for the viewer's eyes. Sometimes I use colour and texture in what I consider a painterly way to lead the eye toward a focal point in the composition."

In the vein of music sampling, Matrayek sees collage as a reality remix that fragments and distorts to the point where new meaning is born from the knitting of disparate materials:

> I feel that collage (and the process of making it) is akin to dreams, where the images from real life are rearranged, remixed, and remapped, where space and scale are shrunk down/reduced or expanded/emphasized, but still somehow connects from one part to the other." In writing, it's often the case where a fusion of fact and fiction can lead you to a deeper truth than either approach could on their own. Similarly, Matrayek believes that "collage can create free associations between images, in a way that can feel revealing of a deeper reality of the world around us – just scrunched down into a smaller space.

And, in the spirit of the amateur/craft origins of collage, Matrayek relishes the often calming and meditative side of the collage process. "Since I am often working on personal or collaborative projects digitally, that takes months to years to complete, giving myself time to make a physical collage is often a reward to myself, to give myself creative alone time that feels different from 'work-work'," says Matrayek. "This kind of collage making can feel akin to crafting, or part of a nesting process of a home."

XANDER MARRO (U.S.A.)

Defining Rhode Island-based artist Xander Marro as a collage animator is misleading. The eggheads would call her a multidisciplinary artist, but she's a freewheeling artist who does puppetry, zines, animation, installations, quilts, and printmaking. She even makes lampshades. There's a definite D.I.Y./Punk aura to her wide-ranging work, and indeed, all of it has imprints of the mish-mashy world of collage:

> I definitely hover between a lot of different media," admits Marro. "I've never been a movie festival person or kind of like dug into that scene. I guess I've sort of always thought of myself as just someone who makes pictures and it was really excited when I figured out that I could make them move.[9]

Marro's wide-ranging interests bring to mind a person we discussed way back at the beginning of this book: Harry Smith:

> I'm a huge Harry Smith fan, even his collecting and the approach of caring about other art forms and being a little bit of a polymath and all over the place, he's just like such an important character. It was looking at Harry Smith stuff when it felt like watching pictures move rather than cinema. It felt like someone putting together compositions and thinking like a painter or something like that too. And I love Martha Colburn. She was influential for a lot of folks.

Self-taught, Marro studied philosophy, semiotics, and film history but always leaned towards art. "I realized that a lot of what I was studying involved a lot of arguing, and I wasn't interested in arguing. I loved art because it could be open-ended, with many possibilities."

Marro's primary introduction to film came via a film lab she worked at from 1999 onwards. Around 2001 she started collecting magazines, and it expanded from there. "The thing that I love is Rhode Island was like the epicentre of junk jewelry manufacturing in the U.S., so I think that what I've loved about collages is mixing in jewels and trinkets. I also love to do paper collages; that's my go-to relaxation activity. What I love about working with photos and animation is that you work with these things that fall off a piece of paper, heavy things like rhinestones and pearls and that kind of stuff."

Marro is particularly smitten with paper collage. "That's my kind of relaxation go-to activity. But the thing I love about like photographing and doing animation is that you can work with these things that would like fall off a piece of paper. They, you know, like heavy, you know rhinestones and pearls and all of that kind of stuff. There's just so much of that stuff in Rhode Island."

When Marro dives into collage work, it's triggered more by just playing around in a studio than having a firm idea. "I make a couple of things and just see what happens. It feels like the most free form of all of the different kind of modes that I work in. I almost never plan anything out."

The bulk of Marro's collage work originates with the material. "There was a moment when I was obsessed with these things you'd get at the paint store that were showing how crackle paint looked. I'd make them into birds or I find some wallpaper that shines in a certain way."

The collage process is a matching game for Marro that often starts as an almost formalist exercise: "It might start with, say, an orange piece of tape. Then I think about what makes sense with that orange piece of tape. It's formalistic, but there's also something magical about it. Everything you're working with already has a life of its own, so you don't have to worry as much. When I'm drawing, I have to think about 'does this hand make sense' or 'is this the right way to be representing this.'"

And it's this sense of freedom and space that Marro enjoys most about the collage process. "It just feels more like play. You get to include the element of discovery while going through stuff; you get to be a collector. You get to be a curator. You get to, especially when animating, be a dancer, as stuff is moving around. You get to think about the relationships between all of the stuff."

L'Eye (2004)

Assorted photos of Italian models with drawn-in eyeballs glare crazily at us before an assortment of patterns jumps into to hypnotize us. The result is a disarming take on surveillance, spectacle, and advertising. Like Colburn's *Evil of Vampire*, *L'Eye* comically comments on the crass hypnotic nature of ads but's also just a funny (well, initially, after a while, it takes on a more creepy and paranoid-inducing vibe) take on a strange and silly gesture we all do.

The Further Adventures of Lady Long Arms in the Land of Love (2004, 11 min, 16 mm)

A grungy cross between live-action, wooden cut-out peacocks and collage materials (shaky eyeballs, photo cut-outs of body parts, teeth, lips, and noses, text clippings) that darts and dances inside the dreams (or nightmares) of a sleeping woman with really long arms. It's like you drifted into a child's head in the early 1970s to see how they see the world they imagine with their toys.

Born to Never Throw Anything Away (2009)

A collision of various collaged materials (jewelry, trinkets, paintings, seeds, photos, strings, and objects) mixed with live-action montage segments of an urban neighbourhood. A wonderfully unharnessed cautionary tale/celebration of *stuff* that carries forward the leftovers abandoned from the dustbins of history. One day we'll die surrounded by crap before we too become refuse.

KATHLEEN QUILLIAN (U.S.A.)

Collage began as a bit of feckless hobby for Kathleen Quillian. "I always played around with collage but not with any intention of doing anything with it."[10] Quillian was already collecting old magazines, books and odd photographs and enjoyed sorting through the materials to see what happens "when you put disparate things together."

All that changed around 2005 when Quillian moved to the Bay Area. "I watched Harry Smith's *Heaven and Earth Magic* with a live band playing. I had never seen it before and thought it was really cool. Then, the next day we drove to Portland for a festival and saw a retrospective of Martha Colburn. The two screenings hit me like a ton of bricks. It seemed like the kind of world I wanted to be a part of."

Unlike many collage animators, Quillian approached her films with a preconceived idea. She spends a lot of time prepping by flipping through assorted magazines and cutting out anything that resonates with her. "I have a huge collection of images that speak to me. Most everything I've made, I have started out with a preconceived idea for one reason or another which is not the way I necessarily wanna work. That's just sort of what happens. I would rather be surprised."

Quillian's approach started with old-school cut and paste until she realized that scanning would allow the original material to remain intact. "In Photoshop I might change the size or colours of the material. Sometimes I create characters out of different body parts. Then print it out, cut it out, and capture it with the D S L R and dragon frame. So I'll be moving things around by hand, but it is captured a lot. There is a lot of digital aspects to it too."

Quillian's films, *Celestial Broadcast for Mrs. Jones* (2006), *Stardust Serenade* (2014), *The Conjurer* (2018), and *Confidence Game* (2018), display a love of mid-20th century advertising photos. Quillian takes these seemingly innocent, clean images and subverts them to explore subjects like mortality, the afterlife, and otherworldly ideas. In Quillian's debut, *Celestial Broadast*, a well-dressed 1950s housewife is vacuuming when suddenly a man/spirit emerges from the nearby radio. Next thing you know, ol' Mrs. Jones is pregnant with a spirit child! In *Stardust Serenade*, a household TV transmits mysterious signals from space, triggering rather unusual happenings. *The Conjurer*, which incorporates old cut-out photos of kids and glamorous dancers, is a nod to magic and the unexplained elements of existence.

"I love advertisements from that era just because they're so expressive and theatrical," says Quillian. "I see them as characters that you can turn into soap opera performers. They're sort of vanilla characters, blank slates you can superimpose many things onto. I think they were probably smoking cigars and yelling at their kids once the camera was turned away. I like to peel under the covers."

Quillian's films are not limited to otherworldly subversions of mid-century America. *Wasteland* uses assorted pirated photos of farms, food, and more modern imagery to interpret a chapter of Michael Pollan's influential book *The Ominvore's Dilemma*. *Fin de Siècle* (2011) uses Victorian images (ala Larry Jordan) to explore her favourite topics: superstition, spirituality, and mortality.

STACEY STEERS (U.S.A.)

Birds fly, spiders dance, bees buzz, bats pester, snakes slither, and strange orbs hatch winged creatures that roam nightmarish dreamscapes as Lillian Gish, Mary Pickford, and Janet Gaynor watch in horror, perplexity, and yet with hope too.

Using imagery from silent films, Eadweard Muybridge, along with thousands of handmade collages, Stacey Steers has created a mesmerizing allegorical trilogy (*Phantom Canyon*, *Night Hunter*, and *Edge of Alchemy*). Within those collage films, she excavates the turbulent mental, and emotional inner landscapes of women thrust into roles and selves they didn't choose. Restless and unsettled, they battle demons of doubt and creatures of anxiety and hesitancy in search of some semblance of self, being, and happiness.

Steers started in animation, creating hand-drawn films before shifting to collage materials. After completing two drawn animation films, Steers had an artistic crisis. "I was finding my style limiting and confining," says Steers. "I was interested in working with more neutral images, stuff less directly my own. I admired the ambiance of Larry Jordan's collage animation and wanted to work in that dreamy realm."[11]

In her debut collage film, *Phantom Canyon (2006)*, Steers uses an assortment of Eadweard Muybridge images to tell a personal story about a relationship between a woman and a winged man. In the film, Steers explores the tricky tightrope of solitude, longing, loving, and independence:

> I started to experiment with collage animation and began combining images from Eadweard Muybridge's human motion studies from the 1880's with clip art of 19th century engravings. I'm a technophobe, so instead of trying to work directly under the camera I made individual collages (usually 8 per second) so that I could reshoot if necessary. The bonus is you get a lot of control over the elements.

During the 4 ½ years that Steers worked on *Phantom Canyon*, she came across several challenges during her first collage effort:

> Lining up the elements was a big challenge when I started this film in 2002. I used a lunch box setup, but you couldn't toggle between images in the early days. In the end, the technique carries a hyper-intensity resulting from flickering all the image elements. The field of the film becomes energized, and it suits my subjects. I've always liked the term 'breathing' for instability in animation because it implies that the images have their own life force, which is cool.[12]

The Night Hunter (2011) finds a woman (played by images of Lillian Gish taken from an assortment of silent films) in a house caring for some mysterious eggs and snakes before turning into a bird. "I was a long time fan of Lillian Gish, particularly her role in *Broken Blossoms*. I was very struck by psychological power of her performance and I thought there might be a way to use her images in collages."

Edge of Alchemy (2017) features silent actresses Mary Pickford and Gloria Gaynor in a mysterious floral Frankenstein tale that touches upon environmental themes.

In the case of *The Night Hunter*, Steers took a DVD of Broken Blossoms (and other films) and then broke it into image sequences of individual frames of action; Steers then cut out images of Gish from the frame or collaged them "into the existing space by laying things over what was originally there, and created collages I could sequence."[13] It was a similar process for *Edge of Alchemy* but with different source material. As arduous as the process is, Steers feels it adds a more personal and intimate feeling to the work. "How you create work," says Steers, "can profoundly impact what you create."[14]

Throughout all three films, Steers creates mystifying dreamscapes that are not just influenced by silent film or Victorian-era imagery. Home (and cinema history) is a recurring theme in all three films, but home is not necessarily a safe, comforting domain. In Steers trilogy, home is an unstable, stifling and often claustrophobic environment, a domestic prison. It's as though

Steers is peeling off the covers of her protagonists and allowing us to glimpse inside their tormented mindscapes.

Steers' pre-collage animations were heavily influenced by Latin American culture. She lived in Latin America for seven years and acknowledged being inspired by "the sense of magic, shape-shifting" that were a constant presence in the culture. Indeed, that mix of magic realism and surrealism is readily apparent in Steer's collage films.

Steers loves the serendipitous nature of collage:

> I like having different fragments and uniting them in ways that are surprising just because they happen to be laying together. I love involving the hand of others in a weird way. Animation can be very isolated and it can be hard to be the generator of everything, so when you start using the found images it can be a frontier that constantly surprises you and the richness of it just keeps expanding. The more you look, the more you find.[15]

NOTES

1 Unless otherwise noted, all of Geiser's quotes are from an email interview with the author, January 2023

2 Unless otherwise noted, all Colburn quotes from an interview with the author, 2022.

3 *Exile: An Interview with Martha Colburn* by Mike Hoolboom. https://mikehoolboom.com/?p=109

4 https://iffr.com/en/blog/martha-colburn-myth-labs.

5 All quotes from Roston are taken from a January 2023 email interview with the author.

6 Unless otherwise noted all of Barcy's quotes are from an email interview with the author in 2022.

7 The Jodie Mack section was initially written for the 2020 Ottawa International Animation Festival. It also reappeared in my book *Mad Eyed Misfits* (see bibliography for details).

8 All of Matreyek's quotes are from a 2022 email interview with the author.

9 All of Marro's quotes are from a 2022 interview with the author.

10 All quotes from Quillian are from an interview with the author in 2022.

11 Interview with the author at the Cinémathèque Québécoise in Montreal, September 2021

12 Ibid.

13 Ibid.

14 Ibid.

15 Ibid.

The Accidental Luxuriance of Recycled Utopian Erodium Pressure Pistols
2010 and Beyond

6

KELLY SEARS (U.S.A.)

"I'm a big proponent of failure," says U.S. animator, artist, and teacher, Kelly Sears.[1] "Failure is a productive force in my work, both in developing ideas for films and methods for animation. The works are responses to failure, of power and institutional structures, of thinking rooted in imperialism and dominance, and drives of capitalistic and technological obliteration. I'm drawn to images that can be containers for some of these structures – and through animation – recasting and reframing new performances of critical histories."

Sears' films explore the flipside of an assortment of narratives that initially spouted utopian promise (e.g. space travel, abuse, climate change, telephone, schools, urban landscapes). Many of her films exist in this alternative universe, which awkwardly fuses material from the past with present prevailing realities. Films like *The Drift* (2007), *Voice on the Line* (2009), *Once It Started It Could Not End Otherwise* (2011),

DOI: 10.1201/9781003214724-6

The Rancher (2012), and *Applied Pressure* (2018) reveal that the boundary line between heaven and hell is a mighty thin one. Above, the grass can appear lush green, but underneath it's full of dirt, worms, shit, and other detritus.

While studying 16-mm film at Hampshire College, Sears discovered the animation stand and optical printer. "It was the first time I thought about working with layers and working, which is very spatial, and working with time and thinking about how time can be cut up and reordered with both of those apparatuses. That laid the groundwork for bringing in different material, cutting it up, layering it, and seeing what new narrative possibilities grew out of that rearrangement. Collage became not just a spatial practice but a temporal one."

Sears is an intriguing collage figure. She's got the spirit of an old-school analogue artist, yet she works with digital tools. "I'm in this in-between place where my aesthetic comes from these early days of working with 16mm film, but my way of thinking through how I can put things together is such a digital practice. And it's one of like, try it again if that doesn't feel right. Try it again and again, sometimes about 50 drafts of one shot before some sort of frequency feel right about it to me."

Her films also reflect this liminal state. Sears approaches animation on a "forensic level. I'm sculpting a frame or a second." Sears films explore those intermediate points between past and present, static and moving, and nonfiction and fiction.

While using found materials from America's past, everything these films speak is rooted in the here and now. *Applied Pressure* is made up of imagery taken from massage and body books. "I picked up an instructional massage book because I love the sequential images there. There are these beautiful, ready-made animations in a way and or blueprints for them, animate by numbers, and you can more bridge them together. The materials sat gathering dust for years. Then all the accusations against Harvey Weinstein and Larry Nassar [U.S. Gymnast Coach/child rapist] came out, and all of a sudden, that book, I knew one day it could be activated."

Massage is often linked with the idea of healing, but in *Applied Pressure*, Sears flips that notion on its back. The sequential movements of the pirated material (that have a red tinge added) become robotic and awkward, with an underlying sense of menace and trauma.

The Drift (about a failed space mission that triggers a counter-culture movement) was created during the occupation of Iraq. I was thinking of George W. Bush on an aircraft carrier in a top gun outfit with a big banner, "Mission Accomplished," behind him. Sears plays off the notion of space travel as progress, as America "spreading democracy."

Voice from The Line used images and archival videos from the 1950s to look at the lure of telephones and communication. Sears made the film during the post-Patriot Act era when surveillance, monitoring, and security issues became prominent (indeed, the theme of surveillance and privacy has since expanded further in the age of social media, Alexa and iPhones).

The Rancher, a faux newsreel film about former U.S. President Lyndon Johnson becoming a tad unhinged by dreams, was inspired by Robert Carro, who authored *The Power Broker* and a multi-volume biography of Johnson. "I love these characters that Carro is attracted to; these really flawed, powerful men with visions who put all this policy in place that's still echoing out today." While in Texas, Sears happened upon an assortment of LBJ newsreels. "I thought of an alternate version of the newsreels. Newsreels always present a very performed daily life and this idea of competence of control. I wondered what a newsreel make up of out control moments or nightmares."

Once It Started It Could Not Be Otherwise is a subtle horror film composed of images from 1970s school yearbooks. Throughout the film, there is this quiet, unseen threat. Something is not right, and will maybe never be right. School, which some (not me) saw, as a place of safety, for acquiring knowledge, now takes on a more menacing vibe. Any number of things could be read into the menace: the uncertainty of adulthood, war, and guns (schools are often a site of gun-related killings in the U.S.A.).

"I'd been to a thrift store and I found a yearbook from 1974," says Sears. "I held onto it and then I was looking at it again and just thought, you know, wow, these, these kids look super freaked out. I was thinking that they're coming of age and they're going into this world of Watergate and Vietnam. Young men being sent to fight a war that was about American imperialism."

Although the film was made in 2011, it's a theme that resonates today. Today's high schoolers have not only never experienced life before the internet, but they are faced with daily worries: pandemic, war, inflation, and all sorts of other concerns and threats.

Sears admits that she needs a "temporal distance" when approaching both the archival materials and the here and now:

> I think about how to talk about a topic, so I time the material with where my head is at the current moment in terms of thinking about what is happening around me. It's always about how I can graft a different story onto these images or make them perform a different story. What if I use something different, like astronauts to talk about the failures of spreading democracy or telephone operators to think about the surveillance of civilians? I've had this distance to think about the present and how we read images that already exist.

Sears' use of vintage photos and film footage also asks the audience to re-situate themselves with the material. "These ideas of trust we have in images will be very outdated. Soon, if not now. I think we're learning how to untether this idea of these images being attached to a sense of authority or legitimacy."

That distancing and disruption that Sears speaks of are also at the core of collage. "I think there'll be more of that in the future, not just in terms of misleading media literacy, but just about any image you even take, you have the option on your phone to share it with a caption, with something you draw on it with a flower crown that you put on yourself. This is a layered way that we present ourselves in the world now, just like whatever basic technology we have."

Where does that leave collage and its counter-cultural roots? If everyone makes collages, won't collage art lose its power to disrupt? Sears isn't so sure. "Every art form starts off subversive before eventually getting co-opted. But there's always these refreshing cycles of doing something wrong that come about continually. That's what makes art really exciting because it's where you're finding these places of resistance to speak to the larger system that's eating everyone up."

LEI LEI (CHINA)

Using a mixed-media approach that combined collage and drawings, Lei Lei's vibrant candy-coloured tales of love and diversity found instant acclaim on the animation festival circuit. Since then, the filmmaker has established himself as one of the most refreshing and unique voices on the animation circuit.

Beginning with the film *Recycled* (2013) and its follow-up *Hand Coloured #2* (2015), both co-directed with Thomas Sauvin, Lei Lei's work took on a new direction. While his earlier films always utilized collage elements, his later work expanded on that by incorporating hundreds of found photographs collected from various Chinese flea markets. In both films, Lei Lei turns his eye from fantasy stories towards a resuscitation of personal stories often suppressed, censored, or erased by turbulent Chinese policies.

Lei Lei's path to animation resembles a collage. During his university years, he was obsessed with underground music. He was also rapping and loved to skateboard. His father was a book designer, which inspired a love of graphic design. Animation became a way to combine all of these passions.

Lei Lei's debut, *This Is Love* (2010), started with music that he composed and then decided to animation so he could visualize it.

From the start, collage elements have been a big part of Lei Lei's films. In those earlier films, though, collage was often a supporting character to a drawn character. Lei Lei would create backgrounds and landscapes using various heisted materials. "I started collage because of my father," says Lei Lei. "He's the first generation of Chinese designers to work with digital tools. My father used collage to create his book designs when I was a kid. He would cut out different colours from magazines or commercial catalogues. He'd write down the title and collage everything to design the book cover. This was a big influence on me."[2]

When Lei Lei started making films, collage was the most logical and natural path. First, there was a personal connection to his father, but Lei Lei also appreciated the efficiency and surprise of working with collage. "When I cut out different material it often gives me a new idea for the story. I learn a lot from the image."

Lei Lei collects black and white photos from second-hand shops, old magazines, and commercial catalogues. "My work is not only based on patterns, colours or textures, but also photos, archives and commercial catalogues from different media. It's a lot of fun but brings questions: how do I organize all these materials together?"

The bulk of the collage materials for his early works came from old book covers. "I cut out patterns from book covers, and I got a lot of commercial book cover catalogues from the 1970s and 1980s from my father."

Despite making several acclaimed and successful short animation films, Lei Lei experienced an artistic crisis in the 2010s. "Attending the Ottawa Animation Festival was important. I had my first films selected there and travelled there almost every year. I remember having strong feelings during the screenings, especially when seeing non-narrative films, that made me question my cinematic language."

Later, while attending a summer academy in Locarno, Lei Lei had an awakening. "We were screening our short films together in a program. I remember thinking that my early films were not strong enough. They felt too short and colourful; they looked like a postcard. Everything felt very flat. The topics were not political, not about social problems or daily life, just very beautiful with good graphic design."

In short, Lei Lei wanted to make films that had some substance. Things started to change with *Recycled*. French collector Thomas Sauvin had constructed an archive of half a million 35 negatives that had been salvaged from a recycling plant near Beijing. For two years, from 2011 to 2013, Lei Lei selected over 3,000 of those photos. Presented as a train ride (each car composed of found photographs, the result is an extraordinary journey that celebrates and resurrects forgotten faces, voices, memories, and landscapes from China's past. Through this resuscitation process, Lei Lei found his voice:

> It's a very important work. I'm looking for my identity or I'm looking for my, my cultural background in this film. I can't find my identity in my early films. They are playful and have a lot of cultural influence from the West, but *Recycled* is the first film where I started to think about who I am. I come from a country that changed so fast in the last 20 years that it has forgotten its history.

Lei Lei and Sauvin reunited for a very different project, *Hand Coloured #2*. Originally an installation, the duo created a fictional narrative using thousands of black-and-white photos found at Chinese flea markets. They re-imagined that all the images belonged to one fictional Chinese person. Through collage, scanning, printing, and hand-colouring, the photos appear to take us through the time and space of a single person. "People threw these memories away, and it's like we are picking them up and bringing it back to the people."

For *Books on Books* (2016), Lei Lei explored both personal and cultural history. The film is constructed entirely from cut-out patterns taken from his father's book, *Book Cover Collection in the West* (1988). The book was published when China was undergoing its "great reform" and opening up to the world. "*Books on Books* is also about my interest in collage," says Lei Lei. "I can't stop making fake book covers in my apartment. I love the bright colours, textures of the papers and the interesting contrasts from the different materials."

Another intriguing collage-driven work is Lei Lei's trailer for the now-defunct Holland Animation Festival. "That trailer is very important to me. It was the starting point for my first feature, *Breathless Animals*." The images in the trailer were taken from a second-hand book from the 1980s that shows Chinese youths how to make quick sketches of human figures. "I cut out photos of the models from the book and placed them in a potted landscape, attempting to discover the occasional poetic and dramatic moment from piecing together the work."

Moreover, the sound in the leaders is a recording of myself, aged 3. It was the year 1988 when I was practicing the violin. It looks like a dream or memory from childhood, except all the material is from a commercial catalogue.

The confluence of memory, dream, and public image is especially intriguing for an artist who lives in a country where CCTV cameras are everywhere (and they are, as I discovered during a 2019 visit to Beijing). "Maybe if you lose your memory," jokes Lei Lei, "you can retrieve it from the CCTV footage. You can find every action of your life on a storage drive."

In his most recent feature, *Silver Bird and Rainbow Fish* (2022), Lei Lei continues this exploration of Chinese history, this time visiting his family roots. Using interviews with his father and grandfather (who died before the film was finished), *Silver Bird and Rainbow Fish* follows the story of 4-year-old Jiaqi (Lei Lei's father). After the boy's mother dies, his father (Lei Lei's grandfather) is forced to put him and his sister in an orphanage while he seeks work in the countryside. Eventually, they are all reunited by a new woman who emerges in their lives.

Straddling the borders of animation and documentary while blurring the lines between personal memory, history, and fiction (many of the photos are not of Lei Lei's family), Lei Lei mixes archival photography, collage elements, hand painting, and clay as he transports us back to a somewhat chaotic 1960s China.

Through this approach, Lei Lei acts as a sort of animation Dr. Frankenstein, patching together forgotten and erased voices, faces, and experiences to tell a story that is at once deeply personal and relatable to many who experienced a similar sometimes-tumultuous existence in China.

Not surprisingly, given the lack of material, most of the archival photos used in the film are not of Lei Lei's family: "Except for the photo album at the beginning and end of the film, the photos are all of strangers. They are photos I collected from second-hand fairs."

This blurring between private and public, family and nation, elevates *Silver Bird and Rainbow Fish* from being a strictly personal family diary. It becomes not just a story of one family but of many Chinese families or anyone who experienced restrictive governments.

The conversations between grandfather, father, and son are meaningful for Lei Lei. "Maybe around 2017 or 2018, my grandfather saw part of the film, but he was in bad health. Later, when I finished the film, I went back to my hometown and watched it together with my father. He loved it. He said he had never watched animation in this way before."

In keeping with the spirit of collage, Lei Lei was also able to create a special moment for his father. "I cut out my father's voice and placed it with my grandfather's voice, so it gives the impression that they are having a new conversation together. My father was very emotional about this part. He said it was very beautiful to bring my grandfather back."

Silver Bird and Rainbow Fish was very important to Lei Lei for various reasons: "If you say *Recycled* is very different from *This is Love (2010)*, then I think *Silver Bird* tries to bring in a different technique. I continue to think about my cinematic language and how to use cut-out and collage together with archive documentary materials. I'm happy I finished this project. It's like a finished promise I made to myself.

MARKO TADIĆ (CROATIA)

All memory is fiction. Fiction is a second rendering of a (possible) event. Then there are the photos and home movies. Sometimes my memories of a past moment are acquired from a photograph or a home movie. I've confused them. Does it matter if my memory of myself is wrong? Isn't it real if I can imagine it, if I can dream it?

That's sort of the vibe going on throughout the work of Croatian animator and artist Marko Tadić (who also represented Croatia at the Venice Biennale in 2017). Shuffling documentary, history, and science-fiction, his films look to the past, but not necessarily a past that existed. In his films, he imagines utopia (*I Speak True Things*), a world with two moons (*We Used to Call It: Moon*), and an unhappy immortal (*Borne by the Birds*). There is a sense of loss, an ethereal vibe throughout, yet frequently Tadić seems to be toying with us because the loss isn't necessarily real, only imagined.

Collage elements are a primary part of Tadić's creative arsenal. Using old postcards, science magazine photos, and various found materials mixed with paint, chalk (which he eventually abandoned for health reasons), and drawings, Tadić takes these disparate elements to create fictional worlds that contain their own internal logic. As with many collage animators, impatience and lack of confidence in drawing skills were motivators for Tadić. "I can make a portrait with you, of course, but it's going to take me a long time," says Tadić. "First off, I don't 'draw' very often, and second, I'm not interested. There are people who love it, but I'm not one of those people. I like things to be quick. I don't want to make a drawing for two days. Taking a magazine and cutting it up made everything faster. That's probably something to talk about with a psychiatrist."

There is also an anti-art aspect to collage. Its violent, imperfect nature takes the piss out of the preciousness of art. "It's not glorifying art," adds Tadić. "It's not oil on canvas or something. It's more about the art process, about finding something out instead of creating this object that will last forever and make you famous."

Nostalgia is another impetus for using collage. Tadić's use of old postcards harkens back to his youth when he collected postcards the way kids like me collected hockey cards. "It's like my daily work," says Tadić. "Going through thousands of beautiful old postcards. I love it. I use this material, and I collaborate with this material. I want to use the postcard directly. I etch away with a pen knife and cut out the image, you know? So, in a way, the image becomes different. Everything is temporary. If I don't use it now for something, then it's going to go to waste in a year's time."

The use of postcards and archival materials enhances his work's mysterious, sci-fi element. Collage allows you to combine images from different times and spaces to create new, impossible worlds. In *Borne by the Birds* (2013), Tadić uses old postcards as background scenery. "There's this 'Socrates prison', there's the fire in San Francisco, there's the earthquake," says Tadić. "The postcards themselves are quite interesting. You'd enjoy them as a slideshow, but animation enhances them and gives them something else to add to their already amazing history."

For *We Used to Call It: Moon* (2011), which was made as a larger gallery project, Tadić uses hundreds of postcards and old notebooks to re-imagine that there was once a second moon before it was removed from our lives. Using the guise of an archive, Tadić imagines what a world with two moons might have been like and how its existence might have been conveyed through collective memories (e.g., kitschy postcards and drawings). Jaunting between fiction, documentary, and science-fiction, Tadić explores and critiques censorship, but inadvertently (the film was made before our world started drowning in lunatic conspiracy theories), it touches upon a society struggling to separate truth from nonsense.

Tadić 's philosophy studies drip through his films. He's not making films to please you; he's making work to challenge you and him. Tadić is especially into philosophers like Plato and Thomas More, who convey their ideas in the form of something like a fable. "I like the narrative way to explain something mind-blowing and interesting and political and literary and entertaining simultaneously," says Tadić. "That's something I kept in my artistic practice. This approach is to try and say something with the work, not to make something nice to put on the wall. But to have like a million postcards talking about the second moon."

KELLY GALLAGHER (U.S.A.)

Seeing Lizzie Borden's classic punk feminist work, *Born in Flames* (1983) sent Kelly Gallagher into a blisteringly pleasant haze. "One of my professors, Jeanne Hall, told me to check out the film. Seeing women on screen, organizing a fight back against rapists, sexual harassers did so much for me as a young 20 something. It was visualizing resistance and that kind of political energy did something for my heart."[3]

Throughout her body of work, Gallagher uses collage as a supporting feature of her unabashedly political work. Animation means to encourage or impart life, or the definition I like best: *the act of being*. In that sense, animators (especially collage animators who work with artifacts from the past) are resuscitators. They revisit and revive the abandoned and forgotten, restoring them from the dustbins of history to not only remember but also contemplate and perhaps question that past towards changing the present and future.

Gallagher's films certainly echo those sentiments: *A Herstory of Women Filmmakers* (2009) is an attempt to visualize the female artists that stemmed from Gallagher's frustration with the male-centric cinema canon; *More Dangerous than a Thousand Rioters* (2006) profiles the life of American labour organizer, Lucy Parsons; *Pearls Pistols* (2004) an aggressive call to arms that incorporates a speech from Civil Rights leader, Queen Mother Moore; *From Ally to Accomplice* (2015) looks at the importance of being an ally to a cause via three counter-culture figures. Even in her deeply personal work, *Photographs from My Father* (2014), Gallagher unearths family stories and figures and tries to mend past and present relationships.

Gallagher's road to animation and collage was long and winding. She graduated from Penn State in 2009 with a film degree. In her senior year, Gallagher stumbled upon animation and made her first film, *The Herstory of the Female Filmmaker*. Made from a clash of drawings and collage materials (photos, archival video), you can feel a vibrant, defiant punk vibe (helped along by the scrappy music of Le Tigre). The idea for the film emerged during a film class when a Professor asked students to name three women filmmakers. Gallagher was infuriated by the question. Her response was a collage animation highlighting overlooked women directors. "I didn't know what I was doing," says Gallagher. "I was finding this joyful home in animation, not fully processing what I was animating. I was making my weird film and had been watching all this Terry Gilliam thinking that I could figure this out. It was D.I.Y., just testing things out and learning for myself."

After graduation, Gallagher sent her reel to many studios, but only a couple responded. One was New York-based Asterisk Animation. Studio co-founder Richard O'Connor offered Gallagher part-time work. Later, after seeing more of Gallagher's lo-fi work, he connected her with Martha Colburn. Gallagher spent half a year assisting Colburn. "I learned so much when I worked with Martha and saw her process. There's a generosity that some artists have that's so special."

Via Colburn, Gallagher was even more inspired to make collage and handcrafted animation works. "The beauty of collage animation is that it feels accessible and inclusive," says Gallagher. "Someone might see a CGI animation and think, 'Wow, that's nuts, I can't do that,' but when I first watched Terry Gilliam's animations, I thought the process was demystified by simply watching the work. These are paper cut-outs. You can see the cut marks. You can see how things are done. It's inviting in a way."

Accessibility was something Gallagher learned from the late animator and filmmaker Helen Hill. "She was big on community and wanted to make filmmaking accessible for everyone. Some artists are very secretive about their work and don't want you to know. I hate that way of thinking because it makes it so exclusive. We'd have many more interesting stories from folks with different lived experiences if we created more access and shared our practices and processes with others."

Gallagher's life took a brief detour from animation. After working with Colburn in Philadelphia, Gallagher worked as a union leader in Wisconsin and Portland before heading back to Philadelphia and working as a cocktail waitress while trying to find her way back to animation and art.

The impact of Gallagher's union experience on her animation is readily apparent. Her subsequent films all focus on introducing viewers to various labour and civil rights figures and movements. Gallagher's approach is refreshing. So often, even the radical left has a stench of masculinity and violence, but for Gallagher, it was essential to show that militancy can be feminized. She achieves this not merely by focusing on radical women but by using flowers and glitter, materials you wouldn't normally associate with revolt. "it's trying to show that radical struggle against capitalism can look feminized. Marylyn Buck, who Gallagher celebrates in *From Ally to Accomplice*, was an imprisoned Marxist who wrote poetry about wild poppies and flowers. It was so nice to pull that imagery in and get us to think differently about what struggle might look like because we'd been given such specific symbology and imagery around those things."

Collage is an ideal technique for Gallagher's work because of its honesty. "When you point your camera somewhere or edit something, you're making a choice. Collage makes apparent this mediation and how it came together. It lays it all bare. So for me, collage is a very honest image because you can see that I'm intentionally bringing together these different elements, like a mishmash. You can see that I've chosen to bring these together. It gives agency to the viewer, creates a space where they can create meaning from what they're seeing."

Despite the explicitly political nature of her work, Gallagher is adamant that she's not trying to recruit or change an audience's perspective. "I think some filmmakers are and that's fine. There was this anarchist theorist, Joel Olsen, who talked about drawing a line in the sand so that you can see if you want to fight to change the world and make it better. It's helpful to see who's on your side because fighting to make things better is exhausting work."

DALIBOR BARIĆ (CROATIA)

In a relatively short period, Croatian animator, Dalibor Barić has created a range of 100 films (of which *Accidental Luxuriance of the Translucent Watery Rebus,* an experimental animation feature, is possibly the most known work). Given the number of films he's made, it's no wonder that Barić says, "I'm not into collage anymore, at least not in the way I was ten years ago when most of my films came out. I was mixing collage with other things like 3D and hand-drawn, But the essence of it is lost, so I feel like some post-new wave band that started the 1980s as a punk band but by the end of the decade became a pop act."[4]

A fusion of William S. Burroughs, Jean-Luc Godard, and Lewis Klahr, Barić's body of work is an impressively eerie, psychedelic, provocative, and head-scratching collision of ephemeral films, Hollywood film, horror and sci-fi. At times – especially in films like *I Sing the Body Electric, Horror of Dracula* (2011), *Spectres of Veronica* (2011), *Transparent Sheets with Virus Perforations like punch cards Passed Through The Host on The Soft Machine, and Persistence on The Beach* – you feel as though you're roaming through a mind in the process of trying to unclutter a mess of memories and experiences, the real and unreal, and inner and outer. Imagine putting together a puzzle using only pieces from disparate puzzle sets. That's the vibe in some of Barić's dense collage work. Along the way, Barić's work addresses themes of power, identity, materialism, and authenticity, along with notions of time, space, and the effects of technology on human existence.

For Barić, collage began simply as play. "On the surface, it was cheap, fast and effective. I needed a fast, straightforward process with no delay or lag, with no time to overthink. It has to be faster than the rational mind. I am a ringleader for a flea circus comprised of found footage, collage and references attempting to make films that examine various subjects."

Barić often started a film in the evening and would finish the whole movie without any idea or screenplay. "When I revisit those collage movies, there's something crazy and untangible in them, as if they were made by themselves, like a ghosts."

Somewhat of an anomaly – at least in the context of this book – Barić's collages are all digitally created. His collage materials come from everywhere: photos, illustrations, movies, recipes, and candy wrappers. "I will collect the weariest, most damaged versions of old movies, where the analogue and digital glitches live happily ever after," says Barić. "I was so excited with the idea of memory – personal and collective – with ghosts, spectres, and hauntology. Film itself is the ultimate ghost or undead. I'm still fascinated with that aspect of the movie medium as if it were invented only yesterday."

Given the strong whiff of science-fiction/apocalyptic elements in Barić's work, it's not surprising that one of his early influences was the aforementioned William S. Burroughs. "My first major influence came from his cut-out and fold-in technique," says Barić. "It generally helped me to try to articulate some of my thoughts into the text, poetry or whatever that could be."

While we've heard other collage artists talk about how they loved the accessibility of collage and the sense that anyone could do it, Barić seems to appreciate the camouflage nature of collaging. "I think that approach provided me with a hideout or mask under which I could operate with my insecurities. Since collage materials are already a finished product, when you connect them pieces together they already look good, so I think I cheat a little bit to avoid my own artistic exposure. So instead of being me, I was the man behind the curtain."

Barić's use of collage also harkens back, in some ways, to the cubists. "You can juxtapose several different things at once that can contradict, challenge or ignore each other. You can show different perspectives simultaneously. Just as comics are a medium are 2D mock-ups of a 4 dimensional universe, collage can show something more than the linear full frame feature film."

Collage art emerged during turbulent times: war, death, atrocities, depression, etc. Barić (like Marko Tadić) comes from a country that also experienced war, notably the destruction of Yugoslavia. How much of the chaos surrounding these artists led them to use a technique built on collision and confusion? "There might be a link, but I think the essence of the 20th-century humans was collage. Big cities, bursts of technological progress, migrations, mediasphere, discontinuity, Einstein's relativity, Quantum physics, Psychology etc. Mid-20th century modern human is a fragmented cyborg."

Throughout Barić's work – and really, we could say this of all collage animation – there is a disruption of space and time. It's not just a collision of past, present, and future, but between inner and outer, personal and public realities. Everything and everyone tossed together. You're anywhere, somewhere, and yet nowhere. Today, tomorrow, and yesterday too. You're now but also *then*, yet *never*. As Barić writes of *Amnesiac on the Beach*, "there is a place where no one exists anymore, and everyone is just their own hallucination on the verge of disappearing."[5]

While there is a tendency to be swayed by the potential nostalgia of collage materials, Barić wants nothing to do with it. "Nostalgia is something easy to manipulate people's emotions with. I view the past differently, not as something pleasant and secure, but unpredictable, dangerous and as something that is neither dead neither live, something which haunt us. You are moving forward by looking into rearview mirror."

Barić's freewheeling use of almost anything and everything he finds online leads to a question we still need to raise in this book: authenticity and originality. Collage is created using ready-made materials created by many "ghosts." As my late Aunt once whispered to me in a psychologist's waiting room many years ago: "Christopher, you ain't gonna find nothing you ain't seen already under the yellow ball of fire that reins down about us."

That old chestnut may be exaggerated, at least according to Barić: "Appropriated materials are something between garbage and our (mass) cultural legacy, so we recircle it, reshuffling, juxtaposing it, making a new connection between seemingly unrelated materials, seeing things from a different angle. One of the best things Lewis Klahr said about his work is that he considers himself a reanimator, bringing old images back to life."

So, Maybe my Aunt was wrong.

Also, I might not be remembering our encounter accurately. It might have been a scene from a show I was watching. I dunno. Doesn't matter.

WINSTON HACKING (CANADA)

There is a manic, anarchistic atmosphere to the Canadian artist Winston Hacking's assorted music videos (*Siamese Brutality*, *Burnout Blues*, *Post Requisite*) and non-narrative driven collage hallucinations (notably the award-winning *Erodium Thunk*). Unlike so many collage artists we've profiled here, who are very specific about their steals, Hacking's work is freewheeling chaos, as though – in the spirit of Dada – he's just grabbed armfuls of material and tossed them in the air to see what emerges when they hit the floor. The results are often mind-twirling wonders that seep inside you before you even know why or how.

Hacking's doorway to collage came, fittingly, from many detours and unexpected collisions. He attended Sheridan College but studied not in their famous animation department but in Media Arts. While he encountered an assortment of intriguing experimental works at Sheridan, it wasn't until he started working with Toronto animator, Christopher Mills (who was my classmate the year I attended Sheridan) that Hacking began to find an artistic path.

> I started off working as his assistant editor, syncing video performances. He would wear many hats, shooting his own footage, editing and animating it and doing the colour grade. That's where I inherited this idea of mainly

doing everything myself. His ability to assemble 2D elements inside of a rudimentary 3D space in After Effects struck me, and I think a lot of people adopted his technique.[6]

Collage entered the picture around 2016. "I hadn't seen much collage animation other than Martha Colburn. I had started checking out her work and that's when I started to discover real collage filmmaking." Hacking was attracted by the freedom of collage and the somewhat sloppy essence of it all. "Colburn was not concerned with a shaky camera. She embraced the shake." Hacking was also fascinated by the frenetic movement in Colburn's work "I learned that you could create humour through pairing photos that shouldn't go together along with limited character movement."

Initially, Hacking embraced collage and animation as a way of amusing himself. "It was almost like channeling high school sketching. It was also about my inability to do any other type of art!"

Another serendipitous moment happened when Hacking moved in with a ground of noise band musicians. "That was my real film school. My one roommate Jon Shapiro worked at Queen Video and he had a ton of VHS tapes and DVDs. He was bringing in underground films and things that I'd never seen."

Another roommate Andrew Zukerman ran a small record label that created its show posters and packaging:

> It was all collage, inspired stuff. I was starting to see tapes being made with collage packaging. It was crazy and quite beautiful ephemera. I owe Andrew a lot for sparking my interest in collage and influencing my aesthetic choices early on. We would have these collage parties where we were doing dumb collages to make each other laugh, and that's where I was like, 'I can do this and not be intimidated.'

Hacking was working at the Toronto stop-motion studio Cuppa Coffee. "TV animation felt so rigid and it wasn't something that I had the patience for." Collage animation, on the other hand, was more liberating. "You don't need storyboards. I can let one thing lead to another. envisioned animations where it felt like you were seeing a live stream of my thoughts. You're seeing the collages being assembled while you're watching it in full."

Hacking started experimenting with collage using a piece of green card and shooting random cut-out elements against it in live action. I'd take a cut-out photo of an arm and cut it slightly at the joint creating a hinge of sorts. I would tape the hand down and pull the bicep so it would get this weird kind of tension and movement. After filming that movement I would now have a moving arm element. I would repeat this process with various cut-outs until I had all of these moving elements I could collage together once I keyed out the green. It was an unplanned, exquisite corpse of retimed movements creating the illusion of a cohesive composition.

A surprise to many, Hacking's collage materials are cut up the old-fashioned way. "They're all from magazines and being put down onto a piece of green card. Then I film it with my digital camera and work with it in after effects."

Siamese Butterfly (2015) is a music video for the now-defunct punk band, Soupcans. A woman weight lifts with a wrench. Another woman rubs her body against a shark, and a Sheriff's head rises and falls out of his coat. An assortment of characters play a version of hide and seek before the song and images explode into a seemingly random collision of collages (primarily a variety of paper cut-out ad photos from magazines). If you have no idea what it all means, neither does Hacking. "I was throwing a bunch of my collages in a shredder when they called. I listened to the music as the collages were being destroyed, and that's how the concept was born."[7]

Hacking made the video in about a month, then it caught the eye of Vimeo, and suddenly other opportunities emerged. Hacking is particular about who he works with though. "I've tried to set it up so I don't generally pitch on music videos. I think that's a scam. It's like people getting you to do free work, browsing through your creative labour without committing to collaboration."

Hacking prefers direct contact with the artists. One of those was the producer Flying Lotus (aka Steven Ellison). "I reached out to him online and he responded. He was basically just asking me to do my thing and I would write up a description or I'll actually just do some Photoshops of some collages to give a preview of what the video could look like."

For Washed Out's song, *Burn Out Blues* (2017), Hacking, never one to repeat himself decided to print his collage materials onto fabric. "I spent probably a third of the budget digitally printing onto fabric, and then cutting out the fabric pieces and pulling them through a fabric green screen, so you get all this kind of stretchy or bouncy effect. My wife had the great idea to use a blow dryer underneath the fabric and to achieve some unusual movement."

The result is wavy, fragile imagery that is continually pulled or "sucked" out of each scene as new collages replace it before they too are inevitably "sucked away." It's an extraordinary work that has often, to Hacking's delight, fooled many viewers. "Everybody thought the video was digital and that I used a 3d computer effect. That's the highest compliment."

In terms of selecting collage materials, Hacking says it's all subconscious. "For me, the content could be a combination of anything that my brain identifies as the right piece for these uncanny puzzles I'm making. It's really about building something new from these old fragments of photography."

Erodium Thunk (2017) was Hacking's first non-music video work. The film was commissioned for a group show (named after Michael Snow's 1956 film, from A to Z). It's a mind-bending piece that feels like you've wandered into the mind and memory of a child from the 1970s or 1980s littered with fragments of magazine ads and TV commercials. Each ad image is disrupted by pieces of other ads, creating this warped and surreal imagery that combines nostalgia and satire. Hacking takes safe, familiar pictures and savagely alters them with all sorts of strange and surreal image interruptions.

"It's like a quilt of video quilts," says Hacking. "I shot one clip and then had all these videos downloaded (I used to compulsively collect video clips). I worked in a non-linear way where one idea would spawn another, not knowing what would happen next.

> I will regret saying this, but I don't know what I'm doing. I like having my guard down and being surprised by the outcome of play.

I made the whole visual and then Andrew, the person I lived with, who initially got me into collage. He is the guy that does the soundtrack. He did the soundtrack afterwards, and I'm sure he was like, can you just like, man, everything's moving so quickly. Can you give me a little bit of space? Like he's somebody who is teaching me that nothing is good sometimes too.

The video for Animal Collective's song, *We Go Back* (2022, co-directed with Michael Enzbrunner), is yet another extraordinary piece of collage work. Hacking recalls seeing Enzbrunner scanning objects while working on his film *Death Van* at the Toronto Animated Image Society [TAIS]. "I had his scanning technique in the back of my head and found this app where you can scan anything with your phone and turn it into a 3D object. It's like an instant 3D collage cut out."

And since Hacking discovered the idea via Enzbrunner, he might as well collaborate with them. "I knew from watching his work that we could work together. And it was so easy to work together."

Using the 3D scanning app, Hacking scanned toys, garbage, and other random items. He then handed it off to Enzbrunner, who composed the scanned materials in Blender. "He would create a camera move for the entire video, and then we would go back to various sections and see where we could fit in new collage jokes, illusions, etc. The camera moved through our 3D maze of scanned elements. So he created this 3d maze out of all these things that I created as collages and scanned."

Hacking found many photographs from a non-profit reuse place called Scrap PDX. "You can buy people's old photographs. I used one portrait of a woman from the mid-1960s and then had a toy dinosaur bursting out of it. But that's like someone's granny. It just goes to show that you don't know where photos will end up. And to be able to keep recycling these things, giving them a second life, is a part that thrills me."

Hacking's work seems to capture the essence of collage – fucking with pre-existing images and materials. It's that very nature that, for Hacking, keeps the rebellious spirit of collage burning. "It's a certain type of person that wants to deconstruct and mess with photographs. Some artists are more serious about collage as an art form, and that's important, but I'm not one of them. I'm doing it for myself and trying to discover new collage techniques. That's what keeps me going."

In an age where we're bombarded with altered and distorted imagery, it's like we're living in a nightmarish collage with no apparent beginning or end.

"I'm hoping," says Hacking, "that the work I create is taking them out of the nightmare."

NOTES

1 Kelly Sear's quotes are from a 2022 interview with the author.
2 All of Lei Lei's quotes are from a 2022 interview with the author.
3 All quotes from Gallagher are from a 2022 interview with the author.
4 Interview with the author, January 2023.
5 https://bonobostudio.hr/en/distribution/amnesiac-on-the-beach.
6 Unless otherwise noted, all of Hacking's quotes are from a 2022 interview with the author.
7 https://www.dezeen.com/2015/11/28/winston-hacking-music-video-soupcans-siamese-brutality-paper-puppets-animation/.

Are We All Just Collages?

7

We've reached the end of our collage speed dating session. I've taken you around the room to quickly introduce you to the guests so you can meet them and get to know them a wee bit. I leave it to you to decide whether you want to get to know them on a deeper level. Meanwhile, I hope this book will serve as a wonky springboard for further exploration into collage animation (especially issues of copyright, authenticity, or expanded animation that I have barely skimmed within this word collage).

Maybe it's owing to having spent the last few years drenched in collage imagery, but I'm left wondering if we all aren't all talking, walking, breathing, and farting collages? How much of our daily words, reactions, dreams, movements, and gestures are borrowed (consciously or unconsciously) from experiences around us? How many of our hopes and expectations in life are (mis)formed by movies, television, mass media, or those around us: friends, family, and colleagues (whose experiences have also been informed by many of those same influences)? Even what we wear is a collage: pants from here, shoes from there, earrings from over there. Each item brought from the original context to a new landscape.

Time out of mind. That phrase has accompanied me for years. It comes from Bob Dylan, a collage artist himself. In the song "I Contain Multitudes" (a title that comes from a poem by Walt Whitman), Dylan sings, "today, tomorrow, and yesterday too." That's how I think of collage. As I wrote in the previous chapter, collage is an intersection of past, present, and future, between inner and outer realities, static and moving, and private and public. Everything and everyone is tossed together into a scrumptiously scary stew. You're anywhere, somewhere, and yet nowhere. You're now, *then*, yet *never*. Our entire life is a collage, a puzzling pastiche, a mix and match, a beautiful and ugly buffet of sights, thoughts, and sounds that resonate long after we're dust. Ain't that somethin'?

DOI: 10.1201/9781003214724-7

Bibliography

Ades, Dawn. *Photomontage*. London: Thames and Hudson Ltd, 2021.

Bergson, Henri. *An Introduction to Metaphysics*. New York and London: G. P. Putnam's sons, 1912.

Birnie, Ian. *Collage and Cut-Out*. Ottawa: Ottawa International Animation Festival, 1976.

Burford, Jennifer L. *Robert Breer*. Paris: Éditions Paris Expérimental, 1999.

Cran, Rona. *Collage in Twentieth-Century Art, Literature and Culture*. London & New York: Routledge Press, 2022.

Elliott, Patrick. *Cut and Paste – 400 Years of Collage*. Edinburgh: National Galleries of Scotland, 2019.

Etgar, Yuval (ed.) *The Ends of Collage*. London: Luxembourg & Dayan, 2017.

Gehman, Chris & Steve Reinke (eds.) *The Sharpest Point: Animation at the End of Cinema*. Toronto: YYZ Books/Ottawa International Animation Festival/ Images Festival, 2005.

Gilliam, Terry. *Gilliamesque: A Pre-posthumous Memoir*. New York: Harper Design, 2016.

Igliori, Paola (ed.) *American Magus: Harry Smith*. New York: INANDOUT PRESS, 1996.

Iványi-Bitter, Brigitta. *Kovásznai: A Cold War Artist: Animation, Painting, Freedom*. Budapest: Kovásznai Research Center Foundation, 2016.

Johnston, Andrew R. *Pulses of Abstraction*. Minneapolis, MN: University of Minnesota Press, 2020.

Kuenzli, Rudolf (ed.) *Dada*. London/New York: Phaidon Press, 2015.

Lavin, Maud, Annette Michelson, Christopher Phillips, Sally Stein, Matthew Teitelbaum & Margarita Tupidsyn. *Montage and Modern Life: 1919–1942*. Cambridge: The MIT Press, 1992.

McSorley, Tom & Chris Robinson (eds.) *The Corners Are Glowing: Writings from the Ottawa International Animation Festival*. Boca Raton: CRC Press, 2023.

Robinson, Chris. *Animators Unearthed*. New York: Continuum Press, 2010.

Robinson, Chris. *Mad Eyed Misfits: Writings on Indie Animation*. Boca Raton: CRC Press, 2022.

Stephenson, Ralph. *The Animated Film*. London: The Tantivy Press, 1981.

Taylor, Brandon. *Collage: The Making of Modern Art*. New York: Thames and Hudson, 2004.

Woodworth, Mark. *Bee Thousand*. New York: Continuum Press, 2011.

Index

Printed in the United States
by Baker & Taylor Publisher Services